THE
PLANET-GIRDED
SUNS

Sylvia Louise Engdahl

THE PLANET-GIRDED SUNS

MAN'S VIEW OF OTHER SOLAR SYSTEMS

drawings by Richard Cuffari

ATHENEUM 1974 NEW YORK

Library of Congress Cataloging in Publication Data

Engdahl, Sylvia Louise.
The planet-girded suns.

SUMMARY: Surveys theories and speculations on the
possibility of life on other planets throughout history and
discusses current scientific thinking on this subject.
1. Life on other planets. [1. Life on other planets]
I. Cuffari, Richard,   illus. II. Title.
QB54.E57   574.999   73-84825
ISBN 0-689-30135-9

Published simultaneously in Canada by
McClelland & Stewart, Ltd.
Manufactured in the United States of America by
Halliday Lithograph Corporation
West Hanover, Massachusetts
First Edition

This book is dedicated to all who have asked whether I really believe that there are people on the planets of other suns.

The clear galaxy
Shorn of its hoary lustre, wonderful,
Distinct and vivid with sharp points of light,
Blaze within blaze, an unimagin'd depth
And harmony of planet-girded suns
And moon-encircled planets, wheel in wheel,
Arch'd the wan sapphire. Nay, the hum of men,
Or other things talking in unknown tongues,
And notes of busy life in distant worlds
Beat like a far wave on my anxious ear.

—Alfred, Lord Tennyson
Timbuctoo (1829)

FOREWORD

During the past few decades, the idea of inhabited worlds beyond our solar system has moved out of the realm of mere speculation and into that of scientific theory. Many people are not aware of the extent to which science now accepts this concept. If they have not happened to read recent books on this subject, they may not realize that most modern scientists believe that extrasolar worlds do exist. They are even more surprised to hear that the existence of intelligent life on such worlds is considered probable.

Scientists have no certain knowledge yet. Since planets of other suns cannot be seen with our largest telescopes, there is no direct proof that any stars have them. Nevertheless, today's theories of cosmology and astrophysics—unlike those current earlier in this century—lead to the conclusion that for a star to have planets is not at all unusual. New information about

3

biochemistry indicates that life too may be widespread, and statistics show that if it is, on many worlds it must have evolved at least as far as it has on ours. The topic of extraterrestrial intelligence is receiving more and more serious attention, not only from scientists, but from philosophers and religious leaders.

But surprising though this is to some, a still greater surprise to most people of today is the fact that belief in inhabited extrasolar worlds is not really new. The idea was not, as is commonly believed, invented by science fiction writers. On the contrary, it was accepted by the majority of educated people from the late seventeenth century until the early twentieth century. Scientists, philosophers, clergymen and poets wrote a great deal about it. When in the 1850's the head of a well-known college wrote a book suggesting that there might *not* be other inhabited worlds, he published it anonymously because he felt it might damage his reputation—and indeed, most of the book's many reviews were disapproving. A prominent university's magazine declared that plurality of worlds was a subject on which "until now it was supposed that there was scarcely room for a second opinion."

This fact does not appear in history books. The information is to be found mainly in the books and magazines of past centuries. Famous authors of those eras sometimes mentioned their belief in other worlds, but they spoke of it briefly and casually, thinking it too commonplace an idea to merit much discussion. The writers who went into detail about it are no longer famous. Their books, many of which were best-sellers in their time, have been nearly forgotten. They remain in the collections of large libraries, rarely called for, in some cases with bindings so old and brittle that they fall apart in one's hands when one first opens them to read.

Such books are not science fiction. Some are "popular science" works; others are religious ones, reflecting their authors' conviction that God would not have created the stars merely for people on this one small planet to look at. All contain speculation about the inhabitants of other planets that was intended to be taken seriously. Readers did not laugh at speculation of that kind, for none of it—even the portions concerning life on the moon —was contrary to the science of its time. Later scientists, who

4

knew more, looked upon it with scorn. Several generations, the generations that came of age during the years between the two world wars, got the impression that science had always laughed at talk of "space people" and that it always would; only recently have respected authorities begun to speculate again.

The speculations in old books, and in most modern scientific ones, have nothing to do with UFO's. The question of whether there are inhabited worlds elsewhere in the universe is separate from the question of whether or not any of those worlds' inhabitants have ever visited our world. Nonfiction of past centuries about extrasolar planets does not mention such a possibility. The idea did not occur to people until about the time of World War II. Since then, many men—some of whom are scientists—have investigated records of strange objects seen in the past, and have suggested that these might have involved alien visitors. But science considers the *existence* of other civilizations far more probable than the notion of their representatives' having come here. And during the former period when almost all educated people were utterly convinced that superior civilizations exist, actual contact between the ones of different solar systems was not even imagined.

Searching for the old writings about extrasolar worlds is a little like a treasure hunt: one cannot predict just where they will be found, and one must look in many places without finding anything. Libraries have reference tools that help, but these tools are only a beginning; often they provide merely clues leading on to other clues. Occasionally one is led to a dead end, such as a work of which the only existing copy is in an inaccessible museum. Yet an astonishing number of relevant volumes are available. One can go to a library shelf, take down a magazine printed over a hundred years ago and turn to an article that thousands of people must have read when it was new—and that nobody, perhaps, has looked on in this century. The wording of the article may seem quaint, and its author may have been ignorant of facts that are now known, but the idea expressed is often closer to what scientists are saying today than to what they said when one's parents were young.

5

There are many current science books about extraterrestrial life. This, however, is not a science book. It is the history of an idea. Not all men and women with important ideas are scientists; science studies only that which can be systematically observed. Long before the invention of the telescope made it possible to observe distant parts of the universe—long before the belief in other worlds became popular—there were men who thought about what might lie beyond Earth. Some had followers, but others were ridiculed or persecuted and at least one was put to death for his theories. Since that time more facts about the universe have been learned; present views of far-off solar systems have scientific foundation. Still, the question of what inhabitants of those solar systems are actually like cannot yet be studied scientifically. When scientists give opinions on it, they are speaking not as authorities but simply as members of the human race, just as their predecessors did. They are expressing not proven truths, but thoughts. This book is the story of mankind's thoughts about the worlds of other suns: past thoughts, present thoughts, and thoughts that will be investigated in the future.

Thoughts about the unknown concern not only science, but religion. For many centuries all speculation about astronomy was inseparable from religion, since the mysteries of the heavens could be explained only in religious terms. Today, when more scientific data can be obtained, there seems to be a firm line between the two. This does not mean that astronomers of today have less religious faith than those of the past. Some do, and others do not. In the past, however, people who drew a line between religion and other affairs placed the subject of other worlds on the ''religious'' side of that line, while it now usually falls on the ''scientific'' side. Unlike their predecessors, modern scientists who believe that the universe was created by God do not spend their time debating about whether the various features of it could have resulted from what they think God must have done; they accept their observations as evidence of what God did do. In other words, they study what exists and form their theories from *its* nature—not God's, which they do not expect to explain scientifically.

To men of past eras such reasoning would have seemed

6

backward. They felt that they knew a great deal about God, and they realized how little knowledge they had of the universe. At first they did not guess that it was possible to obtain more. Gradually, as science did acquire more knowledge, certain ideas about God had to be discarded; and although some people lost faith in all religion when that happened, others came to feel that less had been known of God than had been supposed. They developed new ideas about religion as well as about astronomy, sometimes disagreeing strongly with the established churches. But until this century, few if any people separated their personal religious beliefs from their thoughts about what the universe is like. Even those who paid little attention to religion in everyday life considered cosmology—the nature of the cosmos—too unknowable to be viewed as a purely scientific matter.

That astronomical discoveries came into conflict with the religious view current at the time of Copernicus and Galileo is a familiar fact of history. It is often said that learning that the earth moves around the sun lessened man's feeling of central importance. Many historians, however, feel that the relation between the earth and the sun was not the real issue. More upsetting was the discovery that there are other suns, and therefore, perhaps, other earths—innumerable earths, all of equal importance in the universe. Yet though this was a blow to human pride, before long people began to look upon the existence of countless worlds as proof of God's power and glory. Not everyone agreed with that idea, but by the nineteenth century most religious leaders favored the view that God had probably created inhabitants for many worlds besides this one. Such a faith was shared by people who did not accept any church's definition either of God or of "religion" itself. When no scientific evidence is available, faith of some kind is the only basis for believing in the unseen.

Near the end of the nineteenth century another crisis occurred, one that has not been discussed often. People had been saying for two hundred years that a world would not be created for no purpose, and the only purpose anyone could think of was habitation. Travel from one world to another was not thought possible. So when scientists concluded that the moon and nearby planets are not inhabited, it was natural to start wondering whether the universe is really purposeful. The most common argument for extrasolar life seemed less convincing than before. Furthermore, around the turn of the century a new theory was adopted about the origin of planets. Astronomers began to think that solar systems came into existence accidentally. Such accidents were considered rare; even among people who still viewed cosmology in a religious way, there were many who abandoned their faith in worlds of other suns.

Today, the opposite situation prevails. Scientists believe it is highly unlikely that ours is the only inhabited planet in the cosmos, for they consider solar systems common. This opinion is held by men and women of differing faiths, and also by those with no religious faith. Theologians have again begun to give thought to extrasolar life; most feel that there may be sentient species elsewhere in the universe. Yet the Soviet Union's philosophy of dialectical materialism supports the same idea. A Soviet astronomer has written, "The thesis of the existence of life outside the earth is shared in our epoch . . . in equal measure both by the materialists and by the idealists." There are few issues of such importance on which people of conflicting philosophies can so readily agree.

If life does exist in other solar systems, our view of it is surely important. This book tells the story of mankind's view.

A Note to Readers

In this book, the ideas of men of the past about other solar systems are given wherever possible in those men's own words. Because few reference books mention these ideas, quoting people's exact words is the best way of showing that what is told about their beliefs is authentic.

Some of the wording used by writers of past centuries looks strange today. Some of the spelling and punctuation looks even stranger. Moreover, it does not always seem consistent, for when popular books were reprinted years after their first publication, the spelling was sometimes brought up to date. Libraries of today do not have the first editions of all the works quoted here, although in each case the earliest edition obtainable has been consulted. Practically all of the quotations have been taken from what scholars call ''primary sources.'' That means that they have been copied directly from the book or article the person wrote, instead of being taken from what someone else said that he wrote. This distinction is quite important; the oftener things are retold, the more likely they are to get changed slightly in the telling.

Certain quotations in this book might be a little easier to read if they were changed—but then they would not be the actual words of the man who wrote them. Readers could wonder, justifiably, whether the ideas had been changed along with the phrasing. So no changing has been done. However, because the statements were often long, it has sometimes been necessary to omit portions. The omission of words, sentences or paragraphs is shown by ellipses, or sets of dots, in the middle of quotations.

Actually, if the wording and spelling in the quotations were less old-fashioned, such passages would not seem as interesting as they do in their original form. They would sound too conventional. In many cases, what people of long ago said about worlds of other suns is so much like what scientists say today that only the outdated style reveals how farsighted those people were.

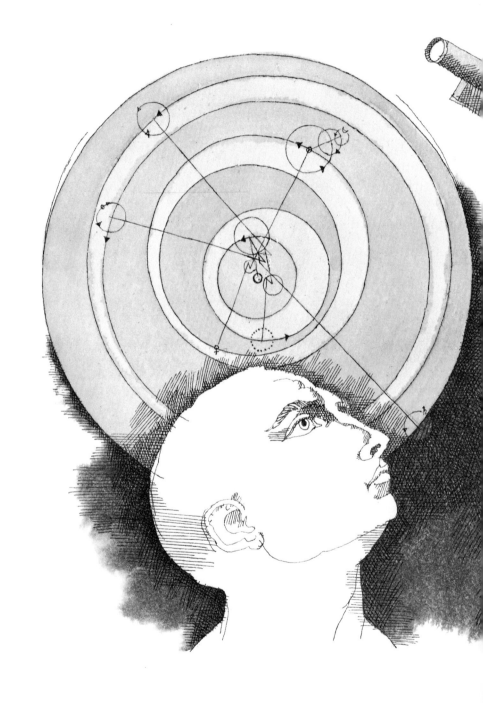

PART I

The Vision
of the Past

Yet is this mighty system, which contains
So many worlds, such vast ethereal plains,
But one of thousands, which compose the whole,
Perhaps as glorious, and of worlds as full. . . .

All these illustrious worlds, and many more,
Which by the tube astronomers explore;
And millions which the glass can ne'er descry,
Lost in the wilds of vast immensity;
Are suns, are centres, whose superior sway
Planets of various magnitudes obey. . . .

Witness, ye stars, which beautify the skies,
How much do your vast globes, in height and size,
In beauty and magnificence, outgo
Our ball of Earth, that hangs in clouds below!
Between yourselves, too, is distinction found,
Of different bulk, with different glory crown'd;
The people, which in your bright regions dwell,
Must this low world's inhabitants excel;
And, since to various planets they agree,
They from each other must distinguish'd be,
And own perfections different in degree.

—Sir Richard Blackmore
Creation (1712)

chapter one

Other Suns perhaps
With their attendant Moons thou wilt descry. . . .
But whether thus these things, or whether not,
Whether the Sun predominant in Heaven
Rise on the Earth, or Earth rise on the Sun. . . .
Solicit not thy thoughts with matters hid. . . .
Dream not of other Worlds, what Creatures there
Live, in what state, condition or degree.

—John Milton
Paradise Lost (1667)

Nearly four centuries ago, on February 17th of the year 1600, a man was publicly burned alive in a plaza of Rome called the Campo dei Fiori. Such executions were not uncommon at that time. Burning at the stake was the usual punishment for the crime of unrepented heresy, not only in Rome but elsewhere; the laws of many countries specified that men and women could be put to death for refusing to believe what the government-endorsed church told them they should believe. This man was not an ordinary heretic, however. He had done more than deny details of the established religion with which he did not agree; he had developed a new view of Earth's place among the stars. His name was Giordano Bruno, and he had written books about an infinite universe containing innumerable worlds. He was the first person to say that there are planets circling distant suns.

13

That view was not Bruno's only heresy, to be sure. Many other accusations, some true and some false, had been made against him, although none concerned actions that would be considered crimes today. There are historians who feel that he was executed solely on account of his religious beliefs. Others, however, are convinced that his ideas about the universe were central to the case. These ideas were thought dangerous; it may well be that they were the reason he was kept almost eight years in the dungeons of the Inquisition in the hope that he could be made to recant. Normally, heretics who would not recant were executed much more quickly than that. It is recorded that when sentence was finally passed upon him Bruno said to his judges, "Perhaps you who pronouce my sentence are in greater fear than I who receive it." Quite possibly that was true.

Why should an astronomical theory have aroused fear in the people of Bruno's time? Why should the church have been so deeply concerned about it? Today it would be classed not as a religious matter, but as a scientific one. Bruno himself tried to keep it separate from church controversies; during his trial he insisted that he had taught only philosophy (as all science was called in his era) and that his beliefs were not opposed to Christianity. Indeed, his vision of an infinite universe was founded on his faith in an infinite God. He had led a tempestuous life, traveling from city to city throughout Europe and more often than not, leaving hurriedly after incurring the wrath of dignitaries whom he had criticized. Yet though he could not seem to stay out of trouble, his deepest wish was merely to reveal truth as he saw it to those who would listen. Most people would not.

To understand why they would not, it is necessary to understand the picture of the universe they already held. According to that picture no worlds existed except Earth; the moon and visible planets were thought to be bodies unlike worlds. This was taught not only by both the Catholic and Protestant churches, but by all the universities. It was the official theory of science as well as of religion. Bruno's defiance of it brought him into sharp conflict with the acknowledged authorities in every branch of learning.

Giordano Bruno is sometimes considered simply a martyr for freedom of thought and speech. But his idea of innumerable worlds was important to him apart from freedom to express it. The idea has since become important to many people. Though Bruno's true role in its acceptance cannot be positively determined, it is known that he was the earliest writer to present its modern form. To future generations this may rank among mankind's most significant advances.

It was not a wholly new idea even in his day. The concepts of infinite space and numerous worlds originated centuries before with the ancient Greeks. Democritus, who lived in the fifth century B.C., taught them; and one of his followers, Metrodorus of Chios, said that for there to be only one world in the infinite would be as strange as for only a single ear of corn to grow in a large plain. However, by far the most influential Greek philosophers were Plato and Aristotle, both of whom were strongly opposed to those concepts. Though such theories were kept alive through various Moslem, Jewish and Christian writings, the belief that there was only one world prevailed.

Bruno had read many of the old writings. Among his favorite books was *On the Nature of Things*, by the Roman poet Lucretius. "You must admit that in other parts of space there are other earths and various races of men and kinds of wild beasts," this book said. "You must admit that earth and sun, moon, sea and all things else that are, are not single of their kind, but rather in number past numbering."

Lucretius had lived in the first century B.C., sixteen hundred years before Bruno. During those sixteen centuries the opinion that the earth and sun were not "single of their kind" was rejected by almost everyone. Saint Augustine and Saint Thomas Aquinas, two of the greatest theologians, were firmly against the idea; and most people accepted what they said. Nevertheless, there were exceptions. Some churchmen declared that the power of God was unlimited and that it was therefore wrong to say that God could not create a plurality of worlds. In the year 1277 the Bishop of Paris officially condemned the proposition that God was unable to do so. These men, however, did not teach that other worlds actually existed. According to the theories of physics then believed, there could not be more than one earth because all the rest would fall to the center of the universe, where our earth was presumed to be. The advocates of plurality merely maintained that *if* God made others, each one would stay where it was placed.

One of the men who argued that there might be other worlds was the Jewish philosopher Crescas. In 1410 he wrote, "Everything said in negation of the possibility of many worlds is 'vanity and a striving after wind.' " But he did not go so far as to say he really believed in them. "Inasmuch as the existence of many worlds is a possibility true and unimpeachable," he continued, "yet we are unable by means of mere speculation to ascertain the true nature of what is outside this world, our sages, peace be on them, have seen fit to warn against searching and inquiring into 'what is above and what is below, what is before and what is behind.' "

A Christian philosopher who felt much the same way was Cardinal Nicholas Cusanus, who, in the year 1440, wrote a book called *Of Learned Ignorance.* Unlike many of his time, Cusanus believed that not everything could be determined by reason, and that it was wise to be aware of one's ignorance. In this book he speculated not only about other worlds, but about their inhabitants. "Rather than think so many stars and parts of the heavens are uninhabited," he wrote, "and that this earth of ours alone is peopled . . . we will suppose that in every region there are inhabitants, differing in nature by rank and all owing their origin to God." He went on to say that there was no way to compare such beings with the natives of this earth. The animals here know little of other species, so "of the inhabitants . . . of worlds other than our own we can know still less, having no standards by which to appraise them."

Cusanus associated infinity of the universe with the infinity of God, as Bruno did; and in fact Bruno was deeply impressed by the Cardinal's book. "This honest Cusan hath known and understood much," he said in one of his own books. "He is indeed one of the most remarkably talented men who hath lived in our world." But Cusanus lived more than a hundred years before Bruno. He did not think of the universe in a physical, astronomical sense; he was more concerned with the idea that God is incomprehensible.

16

Though for centuries learned men discussed other worlds, they never viewed such discussion as having an actual connection with man's place in the scheme of things. It was too abstract and theoretical to be taken seriously. Moreover, very few people had heard about it, for most could not read their own languages, let alone Latin, which was the language all European scholars used. Printed books were a relatively new invention even in Bruno's time.

Shortly before that time, there was a period when intellectual freedom flourished. In the sixteenth century, however, many changes came, among which the rapid spread of ideas through printing was only one. Abstract theories about the universe were not the only topic of debate. People began to question other religious issues too, and that, in some countries, led to the formation of Protestant churches—which in turn led to religious wars and to suppression of heretical opinions by whatever church happened to be in power in a particular area. In the face of this, most thoughtful men feared that further upheaval would occur if the accepted cosmology was laid open to doubt. Besides, they were satisfied with the astronomical system that had been devised almost two thousand years before.

That system is now known as Aristotelian, or Ptolemaic, cosmology, since it was described in the writings of the Greek philosopher Aristotle and was modified by an astronomer named Ptolemy. It can also be called geocentric cosmology because it placed Earth in the center of the universe. Aristotelian cosmology had deep meaning for people. It was not merely a primitive way to explain the appearance of the sky. Its development was a magnificent mathematical achievement, and in addition it involved basic ideas about the sources of human knowledge and the relationship between the earth and God.

In the first place, Aristotelian cosmology was assumed to be correct simply because Aristotle was considered an absolute authority on most aspects of philosophy, including scientific theory. Men of the sixteenth century did not seek knowledge in the same way as those of later ages. They did not expect to discover new things; instead, they tried to acquire and elaborate upon the secrets of the ancients. This was not as unreasonable as

17

it sounds. The ancients, especially the Greeks, had known many things that had been forgotten during Europe's Dark Ages. Most writings of the Greek philosophers had been preserved only in Moslem countries, and when in the twelfth and thirteenth centuries manuscripts were translated from Arabic into Latin and brought to Western Europe, scholars were greatly excited. Aristotle's work in particular seem to them far better than anything they or their successors could ever develop. At first there was a problem because Aristotle had lived before the time of Christ and had therefore made statements unlike some of those in the Bible; but in time Aristotelianism was reconciled with Christianity, and in many cases became a part of Christian doctrine.

During the Dark Ages, almost everyone believed that the earth was flat. The ancient Greeks had known better, however, and when Aristotelian cosmology was adopted the spherical shape of the earth was accepted by educated people with little difficulty. It did not conflict with the basic existing religious concepts; heaven and hell remained in much the same positions they had occupied before. If anything they were less vague; hell was pictured in the center of the earth instead of simply ''below,'' and the location of heaven, too, could be envisioned more specifically. In Aristotelian cosmology, the earth was surrounded by layers of transparent, revolving spheres: one for the moon, one for the sun, one for each of the ''wandering'' bodies—the planets—and an outer one for the ''fixed'' stars, which were thought to be actually fixed and unchanging. Outside the stars' sphere was heaven.

It is important to realize that the spheres associated with this system were more than mathematical abstractions; they were believed to be made of a solid invisible material. Nothing was known of the physical laws that keep planets in orbit, and it therefore seemed self-evident that if the celestial bodies were not firmly attached to something, they would not stay up. Certainly they would not make exact, predictable movements year after year, as they had been meticulously observed to do. Aristotle and the others who had pondered the question of planetary motion were intelligent, ingenious men who had given complex reasons for every detail of their theory. Like brilliant men in every era, they had often worked from false premises; but their logic had been sound.

One of the false premises from which both the ancient Greek philosophers and their Christian successors reasoned was that while things on Earth are imperfect, things in celestial regions are perfect. This assumption referred not merely to heaven in a spiritual sense, but to the physical realms of the heavenly bodies. Thus all such bodies had to revolve in precise circles because the circle was considered the only perfect form; and since no single circular motion could account for the movements of the planets among the stars, planets were supposed to move in many additional circles, called epicycles, within their spheres. The mathematics required to construct such a scheme was extremely complicated. Hundreds of years elapsed while more and more elaborations were added to the geometrical diagram. And that diagram did explain—or *almost* explain—the seemingly erratic progress of Mercury, Venus, Mars, Jupiter and Saturn, which were viewed not as worlds but as small luminous orbs.

Moreover, the idea of celestial perfection went much deeper than the assumption that planets moved only in circles. To the people of the time it was demonstrated beyond all doubt by the sphere of the "fixed" stars. There were no telescopes, and the stars appeared to be constant, unchanging, immutable in a way that no earthly permanence could match. That which was found on earth might pass away. The stars, embedded in the flawless crystal of the outermost sphere, were eternal. So perfection must surely increase as distance from Earth increased; was not hell the center and heaven outside the most distant sphere of all? The permanence of the stars as compared to the wandering planets seemed visible proof of this principle: a principle reflected in the belief that things celestial were of a different *substance* from things terrestrial. They were not composed of the same elements. They could not be, since earthly elements were obviously lacking in perfection.

This was the picture that Giordano Bruno dared to challenge. Certain aspects of it had been challenged earlier; Copernicus, who died five years before Bruno was born, had declared that the sun was in the center of the universe, that the earth revolved around it, and that the movement of heavenly bodies across the sky was caused by rotation of the earth rather than rotation of the crystal spheres. But although Copernicus took a tremendous step forward, he did not alter the basic features of Aristotelian cosmology. He neither eliminated the spheres nor modified the supposition that all celestial motion was circular; he simply found a way to diagram that motion with fewer circles. For him, the "fixed" stars were still fixed. The universe was still bounded by the star-studded outermost sphere. The term "Copernican theory of the universe," which is sometimes used to describe the new cosmology, is not an accurate name, for the Copernican theory accepted by science concerned only the arrangement of this solar system. The theory of the *universe* that brought about far-reaching changes in human thought in the seventeenth century, and that has been retained in its general form ever since, was first suggested by Bruno.

*

The contribution of Bruno is not well known in English-speaking countries. In the Soviet Union he is generally recognized as the first man to seriously believe in the plurality of habitable worlds beyond our solar system. But although he has been hailed by many Western scholars, especially Europeans, as a great and daring thinker and champion of intellectual freedom, his name is far less familiar to American readers than those of Copernicus and Galileo. Popular histories of astronomy often do not even mention him.

There are a number of reasons for this. In the first place, Bruno was not an astronomer. He was a philosopher. To be sure, all scientists were called philosophers in his day, since what is now "science" was then known as "natural philosophy." But Bruno was a philosopher even by the modern definition. He did not watch the stars systematically; he simply thought about them. His theories were based not on observation, but on what he had read and what he was able to imagine.

Because Bruno's idea of innumerable worlds was not favored by scientists during the first half of this century, its significance has been noted only by the few historians with special interest. Usually even they have not viewed him as a major contributor to astronomy. His cosmological theories were inseparably tied to his conception of God both in the sight of church authorities and in his own mind; and many people have disagreed with that conception. It has been claimed that he was an atheist—although actually he was not—and this is another reason why his writings are not widely known. Still another is that some of them have never been translated into English.

However, one does not have to agree with Bruno's religion to appreciate the importance of his contribution to man's view of other solar systems. His belief in many worlds is no longer opposed by the Catholic Church. His vision of a universe infinite in size has been adopted by all scientists for over two centuries, and although most of those outside the Soviet Union now think space to be finite, no one contests the fact that it contains an inconceivably large number of suns.

That was the revolutionary concept Bruno originated. Others before him had suggested that there might be an infinite number of stars. But Bruno taught that stars are suns—or, more significantly in the implications both for his own fate and for the history of human thought, that the sun is only a star.

It does not sound revolutionary today, when everyone is used to the idea; but to people who believed that they lived at the center of the universe, it was an appalling thought. It was much worse than what Copernicus had asserted. As far as religion was concerned, it did not really make much difference whether the sun moved around the earth or vice versa. In either case, the universe—the abode of man—was safely enclosed, a finite creation of God intended solely for man's benefit. Men had argued before that God was surely capable of creating more than one world. That, however, was not the same as saying that he really had made more than one. Although philosophers like Nicholas Cusanus had spoken of the universe being infinite and had realized infinity could have no center, they still envisioned the earth and the sun as special. They thought of the stars as something quite different; most even pictured "other worlds" as being outside the sphere of fixed stars, enclosed within separate sets of spheres. To declare that the sun was a star like other stars, and that the others were surrounded by earths, was far more upsetting.

That the theory of Copernicus was once opposed by religious leaders is well known today to students of history. But that theory aroused relatively little excitement when it was first introduced. The teaching of it was not prohibited by church authorities until after Bruno's execution—more than seventy years after the death of Copernicus himself. Many historians believe that it did not begin to seem dangerous until Bruno associated it with the idea of countless habitable globes.

Giordano Bruno's book *On the Infinite Universe and Worlds* was published in 1584, while he was living in London as the secretary of the French ambassador to England. At the court of Queen Elizabeth I there was much more freedom of opinion than in Europe, for the Queen was tolerant of all religions and enforced England's religious laws only against people suspected of being involved in political plots. Foreign refugees were welcome there.

Bruno had long been a refugee. In his mid-teens he had become a monk; that was the only way for a boy of poor family to get college level education, and he probably did not realize he would come to disagree so strongly with what he was taught. Monks of his time were not permitted to leave their orders, or to disagree with their superiors, so Bruno had to flee his native Italy after it was discovered that he had been reading forbidden books. He lived as a wandering teacher in France, Switzerland and Germany, but he was not on much better terms with Protestant authorities than with Catholic ones. In Geneva they arrested him for publishing an attack on a professor in whose lectures he had detected twenty errors. After similar trouble in Paris the king of France, who liked Bruno, recommended him to the ambassador in England. It was a safer place, although even there he made enemies.

In England as elsewhere, Bruno encountered a great many learned professors who were pompous and intolerant. He himself was not at all tolerant of those he thought stupid, nor had he any gift for tact; rashly, he ridiculed them in public. He was especially disdainful of the revered Aristotle and of anyone who accepted Aristotle's authority. Oxford University was at that time a stronghold of Aristotelianism. The students, who were as devoted to Aristotle as the professors, reacted indignantly to any criticism of him; they took an oath to "drink from the fountain" of that master's teachings, and were fined five shillings for each deviation from them. Understandably, Bruno did not find the faculty and student body of Oxford congenial. His visit there came to its inevitable abrupt end following a public debate with the head of one of the colleges, after which he wrote in one of his books about the way "that pig comported himself." It is easy to see why neither he nor his ideas won many friends in academic circles.

At court it was different; in the house of the French ambassador for whom he worked, Bruno had a chance to meet men who were interested in science, literature and new philosophies. He may have known Sir Walter Raleigh, Edmund Spenser, and —some have suggested—Shakespeare, although it is doubtful that Shakespeare was in London while Bruno was there. Much later, at his trial, Bruno testified that he had met the Queen herself, and it is thought that some of his books were financed by Sir Philip Sidney, one of her chief courtiers.

Bruno's books were somewhat livelier reading for these men than most philosophy. They were written in Italian, a fashionable language, instead of in Latin; and they contained a good deal of scandal. Moreover, they took the form of conversations between characters with different viewpoints. Dialogue was a traditional type of philosophic writing; Plato, in ancient Greece, had used it to record the ideas of Socrates. But in Bruno's dialogues, the characters often resorted to name-calling. Perhaps this was a good thing. *On the Infinite Universe and Worlds* was a serious book and its lengthy arguments about the universe were quite difficult to digest. Was it simply imprudence that made Bruno intersperse passages in which the speakers insulted each other, using terms like "baboons," "donkeys" and worse—or did he want people to keep reading?

However that may be, he expressed opinions about his opponents that were as honest as his comments on their theories—a tactic hardly likely to win them over. Of Aristotelians, for example, he wrote, "Make then your forecasts . . . with which you seek to discern the fantastic nine moving spheres; in these you finally imprison your own minds, so that you appear to me but as parrots in a cage, while I watch you dancing up and down, turning and hopping within those circles."

This was no doubt a plain statement of fact. Bruno's perception of other people's views was less keen than his intuitive grasp of facts about cosmology, and he failed to see that to the Aristotelians, their system of circles really seemed associated with God's perfection. To him such a system diminished God. Further on in the same paragraph he declared, "We recognize . . . a spectacle worthy of the excellence of Him who transcendeth understanding, comprehension or grasp. Thus is the excellence of God magnified and the greatness of his kingdom made manifest; he is glorified not in one, but in countless suns; not in a single earth, a single world, but in a thousand thousand, I say in an infinity of worlds."

Today, the ideas in *On the Infinite Universe and Worlds* have become so commonplace that it is hard to realize how advanced they were for the time in which they were written. The scholar who translated Bruno's words from the Italian used Elizabethan English, which helps to remind readers that Bruno was a contemporary of Shakespeare. Nevertheless, it is easy to forget that people of Shakespeare's era were shocked by them.

"I believe and understand that beyond this imagined edge of the heaven there is always a further ethereal region with worlds, stars, earths, suns . . . though owing to the extreme distance they are not perceptible to us," Bruno asserted through the speech of one of his characters. And another character replied, "You would deny that they are as it were embedded in a single cupola, a ridiculous notion which children might conceive, imagining perhaps that if they were not attached to the celestial surface by a good glue, or nailed with stoutest nails, they would fall on us like hail. . . . You consider that those innumerable other earths and vast bodies hold their positions and their proper distances in ethereal space just as doth our earth."

These were startling concepts, so startling that Bruno himself, who sensed they must be true, did not fully understand them. Because he knew nothing of the physical laws that were to be discovered later, he believed—as did many ancient and medieval thinkers—that worlds were in some way animated. Nothing within his experience could move by itself unless it was alive. That was not a stupid mistake; he was groping for facts beyond his reach, as any daring speculator must do, and the fundamental picture he formed was valid.

The thing that made this picture different from all previous ones was that it was based on other *solar systems* instead of merely "other worlds" in a general sense. Its details occupied many pages of dialogue, of which the following is only a short sample:

Elpino: The proper motions of the bodies known as fixed stars . . . are more diverse and more numerous than the celestial bodies themselves. . . . It is but their great distance from us which preventeth us from detecting the variations. . . .

Philotheo: That is so.

Elpino: There are then innumerable suns, and an infinite number of earths revolve around those suns, just as the seven we can observe revolve around this sun which is close to us.

Philotheo: So it is.

Elpino: Why then do we not see the other bright bodies which are earths circling around the bright bodies which are suns? . . .

Philotheo: The reason is that we discern only the largest suns, immense bodies. But we do not discern the earths because, being much smaller, they are invisible to us. Similarly it is not impossible that other earths revolve around our sun and are invisible to us on account either of greater distance or of smaller size. . . .

25

Bruno wrote this this twenty-five years before the first telescope was turned on a heavenly body, and almost two hundred years before the first planet not visible to the naked eye was discovered in our solar system. No telescope has yet seen any planet in another solar system, for exactly the reason he gave.

Elpino: Therefore you consider that if the stars beyond Saturn are really motionless as they appear, then they are those innumerable suns or fires more or less visible to us around which travel their own neighboring earths which are not discernible by us.

Philotheo: Yes, we should have to argue thus, since all earths merit the same amount of heat, and all suns merit the same amount.

Elpino: Then you believe that all those are suns?

Philotheo: Not so, for I do not know whether all or whether the majority are without motion, or whether some circle around others, since none hath observed them. . . . But however that may be, the universe being infinite, there must ultimately be other suns. . . . Around these bodies there may revolve earths both larger and smaller than our own.

Elpino: How shall I know the difference? How, I say, shall I distinguish fiery bodies from earths?

Philotheo: Because fiery bodies are fixed and earths are in motion; because fiery bodies scintillate and earths do not; of which indications, the second is more easily perceptible than the first.

Elpino: They say that the appearance of scintillation is caused by the great distance from us.

Philotheo: If that were so, the sun would not scintillate more than all the others; and the small stars which are more remote would scintillate more than the larger which are nearer to us.

Elpino: Do you believe that fiery worlds are inhabited even as are watery bodies?

Philotheo: Neither more nor less.

Elpino: But what animals could live in fire?

Philotheo: You must not regard these worlds as compounded of identical parts, for then they would be not worlds but empty masses, vain and sterile. Therefore it is convenient and natural to assume that their parts are diverse just as our own and other earths comprise diverse parts, though some celestial bodies have the appearance of illuminated water as others of shining flames.

Elpino: You believe then that the prime matter of the sun differeth not in consistency and solidarity from that of the earth? For I know that you do not doubt that a single prime matter is the basis of all things.

Bruno made other mistakes there, of course. Suns do move, and they are so unlike planets that modern scientists do not think life can exist on them. But Bruno's reasoning, based on what little information he possessed, was sound. He perceived that "fire" was not a single element, as was thought at the time, but that many elements must exist in the stars—the same elements that exist on Earth rather than uniquely "celestial" ones.

Speaking of Nicholas Cusanus, Bruno had Philotheo say: "As to the apprehension of truth . . . he is a swimmer in the tempestuous waves cast now upward, now downward, for he did not see the light continuously, openly and clearly, and he swam not in calm and quiet, but with interruptions and at certain intervals; the reason being that he did not discard all those false principles imbibed with the usual doctrine from which he had parted." That description could as well apply to Bruno himself, and to all men who have ever striven toward truth unknown in their time.

Truth was of tremendous importance to Bruno; he said a good deal in other books about how highly he valued it. In the introduction to *On the Infinite Universe and Worlds* he wrote: "Assuredly I do not feign; and if I err, I do so unwittingly; nor do I in speech or in writing contend merely for victory, for I hold worldly repute and hollow success without truth to be hateful to God, most vile and dishonourable." He did not always perceive the truth. As a sixteenth-century man, he too believed that knowledge was to be sought in the past: in the work of Greeks still more remote than Aristotle, in that of medieval writers of all creeds, and even in the occult secrets of ancient Egypt. What was new and powerful in his thought was the way he combined the ideas he met there, and the implications he saw in their relationship to the theory of Copernicus. Some historians of science believe that Bruno was too much of a mystic and a dreamer to be counted among the founders of modern cosmology; but the fact remains that he was the first to say that if there was one sun around which planets revolved, there must also be others. Today it seems strange that he had to die for his far sight.

Yet in a way it is not so strange. The world-view Bruno threatened was cherished by his society, a society that had seen the "new" star of 1572 (a supernova) as a sign of impending doom. To that society's representatives all thought of change in the heavens was repugnant. "Where then is that beautiful order, that lovely scale of nature rising from the denser and grosser body which is our earth . . . to divine which is the celestial body?" demanded one of the speakers in *On the Infinite Universe and Worlds*. And he was answered, "You would like to know where is this order? In the realm of dreams, fantasies, chimeras, delusions."

It must be remembered that the question represented the viewpoint of all established authority, scientific as well as religious. For Bruno to answer it by calling the old cosmology a delusion was the same as to say that all the men in positions of respect were crazy. Worse, he was attacking something that people desperately *wanted* to believe in, an orderly system that in their minds was solace for the confusion of life in the world they knew. "In this way, you would put the world upside down," the protestor asserted. In reply he was asked, "Wouldst thou consider him to do ill who would upset a world which was upside down?'' Bruno surely knew that he would indeed be considered to have done ill.

A book like his had a potentially more explosive effect than any political tract. Though printed in England, it bore a false imprint of Venice. Bruno later said that he had been told that this would increase its sales, since Italian literature was popular among educated Englishmen. Scholars feel that the real reason was that the publishers were afraid to put their own name on it.

He wrote other books on cosmology and religion that were equally objectionable to people. He also wrote some on magic, which were less objectionable; magic was quite respectable if not of the diabolic sort. Bruno was often thought to be a magician, and there are a few modern historians who believe that he envisioned himself as a mage, or benevolent wizard. Be that as it may, he sincerely thought he could teach ''magical'' arts of memory improvement: an occupation that proved fatal to him in the end. Six years after leaving England to resume his wanderings, he accepted the invitation of an Italian nobleman who wanted to learn such arts. When Bruno arrived in Italy and proved unable to impart occult powers, this nobleman—who had hoped to acquire more than a better memory—betrayed him to the Inquisition.

It is not known why Bruno decided to go back to Italy. He must have realized that his peril would be great there. However, in the records that have survived of his life and imprisonment, there are indications that he really believed the church authorities would accept his ideas if they could only be made to listen. He considered himself a Catholic despite his disagreement with many of the official Catholic teachings, and at his trial it seems he was attempting to convert his judges to his own way of thinking. At one point, when it appeared likely that he would be condemned for minor heresies, he agreed to abjure ''all errors'' he had ever made; but neither then nor later did he specifically retract any of his beliefs about the infinite universe and worlds. He was sent to the dungeons of Rome; and finally, after nearly eight years, to the stake. An early biographer wrote, ''The report was current among the newsmongers of the day that Bruno said he died a martyr and willingly.''

29

It is easy now to see that Bruno chose to die in defense of his ideas, which might have been forgotten if he had repudiated them. It is harder to see that those who sentenced him were also defending an idea, one they truly believed must be upheld for the good of all concerned. No one can be sure what went on in the minds of Bruno's judges during the years he was imprisoned, but it seems likely that for the first time they gave serious consideration to the concept of extrasolar planets; and the records, though incomplete, do show that he was told to give up his "vanities concerning diverse worlds." Such speculations, combined with the theory of Copernicus, could shatter the barrier that divided the world from heaven. They could destroy the whole view of celestial regions on which religion then seemed to depend. The church authorities who recognized this could see ahead, though not far enough to realize that the enduring things in Christianity had nothing to do with Aristotelian cosmology. No doubt they were less worried over Bruno's ideas about God, which were unlikely to gain popular support in any case, than over those that threatened people's faith in a well-structured universe centered upon God's concern for man.

Execution by fire was at that time an established legal procedure, formally carried out by the civil authorities. The judges of the Inquisition were mistaken in thinking its cruelty justified, but they were not dishonest; and their methods were in keeping with the customs of the age in which they lived: a fact illustrative of the progress that has been made since the sixteenth century.

Today in the Campo dei Fiori there is a statue of Giordano Bruno, erected in the year 1889 and dedicated before a crowd of thirty thousand people who gathered to honor his memory. Most of these people thought of him in connection with freedom of religion alone. Science had earned the credit for proving that stars were suns, and the belief that those suns must have planets —probably inhabited planets—had become so widespread that few recalled who originated it. For Bruno died in 1600, at the dawn of the seventeenth century; and by the time that century was over almost all educated men believed exactly what he had said about the existence of other worlds.

chapter two

But if that infinite suns we shall admit,
Then infinite worlds follow in reason right,
For every sun with planets must be fit,
And have some mark for his farre-shining shafts to hit. . . .

No serious man will count a reason slight
To prove them both, both fixèd suns and stars
And centres all of several worlds by right;
For right it is that none a sun debarre
Of planets, which his just and due retinue are.

—Henry More
Democritus Platonissans (1647)

Historians do not know to what extent the growth of belief in other worlds was due to Bruno's influence. It is difficult to determine because when he was sentenced to burn, it was also decreed that his books should be burned, and people who belonged to the Catholic Church were forbidden to read them. Naturally, some hid copies and read them anyway, but they could scarcely quote from them approvingly in their own writings. Most Protestants did not want to quote Bruno either, since they were equally opposed to many of the religious ideas he had expressed. The idea of an infinite universe filled with inhabited worlds flourished as part of Copernican astronomy; but as to just how it became a tenet of Copernicanism, there are mysterious gaps. Seventeenth-century writers who favored it treated it as a common idea that was already widely discussed.

31

It is frequently said that the discovery that the earth is not in the physical center of the universe was upsetting to people because they considered the center the place of greatest dignity. Scholars who have studied medieval beliefs in detail, however, point out that this is not true. The center was not thought to be a position of honor by Aristotelians; it was the *lowest* place.It was the farthest from heaven and the closest to hell—in fact hell was presumed to occupy the exact center. Furthermore, the earth was supposed to be composed of elements inferior to those found in the celestial spheres surrounding it. Both Christian and Jewish philosophers wrote a great deal about how small, base and corrupt Earth was in comparison to those spheres. One of the things that angered people most about the new cosmology was its assertion that heavenly bodies themselves were imperfect. Galileo, in his first book about his telescopic discoveries, wrote, "We shall prove the earth to be a wandering body surpassing the moon in splendor, and not the sink of all dull refuse of the universe." Such statements were considered by some to be blasphemous.

Most modern historians therefore feel that the Copernican theory was not a threat to man's dignity, at least not at first. Even the concept of the earth's motion served to suggest that Earth shared the "perfection" associated with the circles in which celestial bodies were thought to move. Nevertheless, the cosmology that developed from the Copernican theory—which was often called "the new philosophy"—did strike a blow to human pride. It did so by implying that man was not the center of the universe in a spiritual sense: in other words, that this world is not the only one of importance, and that the universe does not exist merely for man's benefit. In addition, it taught something much more frightening than the removal of Earth from the physical center of the universe. It taught that the universe has no center at all.

Bruno, and other philosophers who speculated about infinity, had not found the idea of no center frightening. The majority of people who tried to envision an infinite universe felt differently. They wanted a neat, orderly cosmos with a plan they could understand. They were deeply disturbed at the thought of space going on and on forever, with stars scattered here and there at unpredictable distances from each other. There are still people today who are frightened by the vastness of space; some of them think that if no clear pattern is apparent in it, then no pattern exists. Some believe that such a universe reduces man to total insignificance. These feelings were far worse among seventeenth-century people, who were suddenly told that the arrangement of things was not as it had been pictured for countless generations. The French philosopher Blaise Pascal spoke for many with his famous statement, "The eternal silence of these infinite spaces terrifies me."

Perhaps that was one reason why the controversy about the new cosmology focused upon the theory of Copernicus. Perhaps people did not like to talk about the other things. The solar system was closer to home, and it was a less upsetting topic of debate. Moreover, it was obvious that if the earth was *not* a planet that revolved around the sun, none of the other issues would need to be raised. Whether or not this was the case (and there is no way of really knowing) the advocates of the "new philosophy" were called Copernicans, although most of them believed things Copernicus had never suggested. Also, their opponents started to place more and more emphasis on the assertion that the movement of the earth was contrary to the Bible: an assertion that had rarely been taken seriously before the full implications of the Copernican theory were seen. However, not everyone interpreted the Bible in the same way, and many people felt that it did not say anything with which Copernicanism did not fit.

The conflict between the old and new cosmologies should not be viewed as a conflict between religion and science. Many scientists were Aristotelians, and they resisted Copernicanism because it was not compatible with the current theories of physics. On the other hand, the Copernicans believed that nothing found to be true could be contrary to religion; they considered truth about the arrangement of the universe as vital to religion itself as to astronomy.

Part of the trouble was that religion, in that era, was mixed up with politics. For more than a hundred years Catholics had fought against Protestants and Protestant sects had fought against each other. Anything that weakened the authority of an established church also endangered the kings who belonged to it. It was a turbulent time, and there were sincere theologians who felt that uneducated people would lose their faith if the church's teachings about the universe were allowed to be challenged. Especially they felt that it was the place of the church to decide what the Bible meant. One of the biggest issues between Catholics and Protestants concerned the right to interpret the Bible; when Copernican scientists like Galileo began to write their own interpretations, they were attacking the church not with scientific fact, but with competition in its own field.

Their attack on orthodox physics was even more audacious. Aristotelian scientists argued that if the earth moved there would be a wind strong enough to blow down trees, that birds could not fly fast enough to keep up, and that the world itself might be torn apart. There were also technical, mathematical arguments backed by sound logic. The unproven assumptions demanded by the new cosmology seemed less justifiable than those of the old. For example, it was correctly reasoned that slight differences in the positions of the stars should be observed if the earth revolved around the sun. Since no such differences could be measured, it had to be assumed that the stars were much farther away than had been thought, and therefore much larger. To many, these assumptions were unnecessary and unreasonable—more unreasonable than revolution of the sky. After all, man's senses proclaimed that the earth *did* stand still; there was no observational evidence that it did not. Nor was there any physical theory to explain its motions, or those of any planet. What caused such motions, and what kept them regular? The Aristotelians had a detailed explanation based on the crystal spheres; the Copernicans, at first, could offer none.

The first scientific evidence for the fact that stars are suns, and that moons and planets are worlds, came in 1609 when Galileo first looked at the heavenly bodies through a telescope. Galileo himself did not believe in worlds outside our solar system—at least he never said that he did. However, he was arrested by the Inquisition for teaching Copernican theory as fact, and unlike Bruno he did recant. He retracted his criticism of Aristotelian cosmology. It has been suggested that his memory of Bruno's fate may have had something to do with this; but the two cases are not comparable. Galileo honestly agreed with the Catholic Church in most religious matters, and he was therefore in the position of having to choose between his religion and what the telescope showed. He knew that the telescope's evidence would not be affected by his denial of it. If Bruno had recanted, his ideas would have been discredited, since he had nothing but his own words to support them. That was not true of Galileo. People went on looking in telescopes despite his recantation, and meanwhile, he was able to complete further important work.

Galileo's book *Dialogue Concerning the Two Chief World Systems* did a great deal to publicize Copernican ideas, perhaps more than it would have if it had not been banned. His greatest contribution to science was not that book, however. More significant was his role in developing a new theory of physics. Among the other seventeenth-century scientists most influential in the development of physics were Kepler, Descartes, and Newton, of whom more will be said later. All these men believed in the existence of other inhabited worlds, but without their work as physicists and mathematicians, their new philosophy of the universe would never have gained acceptance. Only by overcoming the valid objections of traditional science could Copernicanism advance.

As, gradually, it did advance, the larger implications Bruno had seen took hold. These implications frightened people, yet at the same time fascinated them. Not so long before, Columbus and other explorers had discovered a "New World" on the opposite side of the earth. The church had previously taught that there could be no inhabitants there, and had been forced to revise its teachings, a fact that believers in plurality of worlds lost no opportunity to point out. If there were unknown lands in one place, why not in another? To the average man, who knew nothing of philosophers and their arguments, the idea of an "upside down" continent was scarcely less strange than that of a distant planet.

The old ways of viewing the world were too deeply shaken to be preserved. Though thoughtful people were disturbed by the revolutionary new cosmology, many were drawn to it despite their fears. Possibly some who voiced the loudest objections were the most attracted underneath; it is often so when traditions lose their power.

The traditional conception of the universe lost its power to symbolize religious faith. But faith itself was neither lost nor separated from astronomy. Soon, in fact, the idea of extrasolar worlds became a symbol of the wisdom and majesty of God.

*

That change, of course, did not take place overnight. The controversy lasted for many years, years during which steady progress was being made in astronomical science.

It was Johannes Kepler who first abandoned the assumption that all heavenly bodies move in perfect circles. His laws of planetary motion were a great advance. Kepler, however, did not accept the idea of an infinite universe without a center. He was convinced that the sun was the center, and to Galileo he wrote, "From none of the fixed stars can such a view of the universe be obtained as is possible from our earth." He also wrote that he rejoiced that the telescope had not discovered any planets revolving around other stars, saying that this freed him from great fear that had gripped him when he first heard about Galileo's book. Kepler referred to Bruno's belief in infinite worlds as "that dreadful philosophy." He meant, literally, that it filled him with dread, for his own theory of the universe was an orderly one based on a symbolic correspondence between the positions of the planets and geometrical shapes.

Yet Kepler did not lack mental daring. He not only believed that the moon and planets of our own solar system were inhabited, but made the first serious suggestion that man would someday travel to those planets. "As soon as somebody demonstrates the art of flying," he said in his letter to Galileo, "settlers from our species of man will not be lacking. . . . Given ships or sails adapted to the breezes of heaven, there will be those who will not shrink from even that vast expanse. . . . Does God the

Creator . . . lead mankind, like some growing youngster gradually approaching maturity, step by step from one stage of knowledge to another? . . . How far has the knowledge of nature progressed, how much is left, and what may men of the future expect?''

One of the best-known and earliest protests against the Catholic decree that Copernicanism could be taught only as a mathematical calculating device was the *Defense of Galileo* by Thomas Campanella, who wrote it while confined in a dungeon. Campanella, like Bruno, was a monk and had been accused of heresy; but his prison sentence was the result of involvement in political conspiracy. The church did not object to the publication of his book, which was a detailed, impartial analysis of the arguments on both sides of the question that pertained to religion. (Not being a scientist, Campanella did not discuss the issue of physics.) In particular, he pointed out that past theologians had made statements supporting plurality of worlds, and supporting interpretations of the Bible that did not rule out motion of the earth or life on other planets. He did not say that he himself believed any aspects of the new cosmology, but he declared that it was a mistake to suppress such ideas. His book was read and quoted for many years by educated men throughout Europe.

Two other very influential books were written in 1638 and 1640 by John Wilkins, a bishop of the Church of England. They were titled *The Discovery of a New World; or, a Discourse tending to prove that there may be another habitable World in the Moon, with a Discourse concerning the Possibility of a Passage thither,* and *A Discourse concerning a New Planet; tending to prove that it is probable that our Earth is one of the Planets.* These were long books discussing the religious objections to existence of other worlds in detail, as well as the possible nature of the moon's inhabitants. The chapter headings give a good idea of the contents: they include, for instance, ''That a plurality of worlds doth not contradict any principle of reason or faith;'' ''That the heavens do not consist of any such pure matter which can privilege them from the like change and corruption as these inferior bodies are liable unto;'' and even, ''That it is possible for

37

some of our posterity to find out a conveyance to this other world, and if there be inhabitants there, to have commerce with them."

In this last chapter Bishop Wilkins said, "I do seriously, and upon good grounds, affirm it possible to make a flying chariot. . . . The perfecting of such an invention would be of such excellent use, that it were enough not only to make a man famous, but the age also wherein he lives. For besides the strange discoveries that it might occasion in this other world, it would be also of inconceivable advantage for travelling, above any other conveyance that is now in use."

It may seem strange that he imagined moonships being invented before planes and used for air travel as an afterthought. But science had not yet defined the difference between air and space. There was no real need for a "flying chariot" merely to get to the other side of the earth; only passage to another world demanded a means of flight. And while such voyages were sometimes described in fiction, seventeenth-century science fiction was intended mainly as satire. Very few people shared Bishop Wilkins' optimism in regard to flight as an actual possibility.

Although Bishop Wilkins wrote chiefly about the moon, he did imply a belief in other inhabited solar systems too. In answer to the contention that God could have had no purpose for making the stars as large and far away as the Copernican theory assumed, he asked the purpose of stars visible only through a telescope, and said, "Though scripture do tell us that these things were made for our use, yet it does not tell us that this is their only end. It is not impossible, but that there may be elsewhere some other inhabitants, by whom these lesser stars may be more plainly discerned." With this comment, Bishop Wilkins introduced an idea that dominated thought about other worlds for at least two and a half centuries: the idea of the purpose of those worlds.

Under the old view it was assumed that God made everything for the use of man. But actually religion had never taught that man should consider himself of supreme importance in relation to God. The eighth psalm declares, "What is man, that thou art mindful of him?" and this had been pondered for hundreds of years before people began quoting it—as they soon did—in connection with the vastness of the universe. Once the existence of telescopic stars became undeniable, the idea of each star having inhabited planets was quickly accepted. Though there were holdouts against Copernicanism—such as Alexander Ross, who in answer to Bishop Wilkins' books published one entitled *The New Planet no Planet, or, the Earth no Wandering Star except in the Wandering Heads of the Galileans*—everyone who did adopt the new cosmology adopted the idea of extrasolar worlds as an integral part of it. In fact, many who had not favored it were converted by their conviction that stars could not have been made without any purpose.

In general, people felt that an uninhabited world, or a star that gave light to no worlds, would be useless by any standard imaginable. In 1678 Ralph Cudworth, in a book called *The True Intellectual System of the Universe,* wrote, ''Now it is not reasonable to think that all this immense vastness should lie waste, desert, and uninhabited, and have nothing in it that could praise the Creator thereof, save only this one small spot of Earth.'' It was that argument, more than any other, that turned churches from opponents of belief in extraterrestrial life into its most ardent defenders. But religious leaders were not the only ones who used the argument. Scientists used it, too. Without data to work from, their theories were based entirely on their reasoning; and the thought of a useless sun or planet struck them as wholly unreasonable.

Scientific theories of other solar systems took quite a while to develop. Kepler and Galileo, the founders of the necessary physics, concentrated on our solar system alone. Not until the middle of the seventeenth century were the essential features of the new cosmology proclaimed by a major scientist: the French philosopher and mathematician, René Descartes.

Descartes was a Catholic, and although he was also a Copernican, was unwilling to defy the edicts of his church. When he heard that Galileo's book had been condemned, he was astonished, for he saw nothing wrong in it; but he decided not to publish the book on Copernicanism that he himself had just finished. Some feel he was afraid to do so; others have pointed out that since he was a Frenchman and lived in Protestant-dominated Holland he could scarcely have feared the Inquisition, which had power only in Italy and Spain. It seems more likely that he merely wanted to keep his works off the prohibited list. Descartes' ideas about cosmology did not involve the concept around which the religious opposition had become centered. He did not believe that the earth moved; instead, he believed that all celestial bodies were at rest in a moving sky. According to his "Theory of Vortices," which he set forth in his *Principles of Philosophy* ten years after Galileo's trial, all space was filled with invisible fluid matter that moved planets around suns in whirlpool currents. The earth itself did not move any more than do people who sleep aboard a ship that is carrying them across the ocean.

To the modern mind this may seem as if Descartes was trying to get around the opposition to Copernicanism on a technicality. Some historians have interpreted it that way, but there is no doubt that he sincerely believed in the fluid vortices. He had strong reasons for such a belief; philosophers had long taught that a void, or empty space, could not exist, and a basic principle of Aristotelian physics was nature's "abhorrence of a vacuum." The vortex theory of Descartes was the first attempt to provide a physical explanation for the Copernicans' system of planetary motion. Its aim was to remove the main stumbling block to acceptance of that system by science; the fact that it circumvented religious opposition too may have been coincidental. Descartes did not avoid the underlying issues, those more basic to religion than motion of the earth. Though he called the universe "indefinite" rather than "infinite" in size, his system assumed that all stars were the centers of vortices and that all probably had planets. Because this system met little strong hostility from either theologians or scientists, the Cartesians—as Descartes' followers were called—were credited with originating plurality of extrasolar worlds as a modern astronomical concept. The earlier speculators like Bruno were almost forgotten.

Today, Descartes is better known for his contributions to philosophy than to science. Yet his theory was dominant in cosmology for many decades—in some countries, for more than a century. Some have said that its supremacy delayed acceptance of the more accurate theory of Newton; but though this may be true, it is doubtful whether people would have accepted Newton's ideas if Descartes' had not preceded them. The Cartesian vortex theory could not be attacked on the basis of traditional objections to Copernicanism. Furthermore, it could be easily pictured and understood. It was based on a principle that exerted great influence not only on astronomy but on all science: the principle that the universe is like a machine. Mechanism is no longer a tenet of scientific theory, for it is now known to be a much oversimplified view of physical phenomena. Yet even today a mechanical picture is the only kind some people can visualize.

The theory of Sir Isaac Newton, discoverer of the law of gravitation, was less mechanical than Cartesianism. That was people's chief objection to it. The idea that planets were suspended in empty space, and kept in orbit by an invisible force from the sun, was not only incredible to them; it sounded like a step back to supernaturalism. Philosophers, scientists and mathematicians called gravity an "occult" force. They viewed it in much the same way as many still view ESP. That gravity should act at a distance, without any material connection between two celestial bodies, seemed no less impossible than telepathic communication seems to today's most conservative scientists.

Newton's book *Mathematical Principles of Natural Philosophy,* which was first published in 1687, is one of the most famous and important ones in the history of science. It became the foundation of both modern astronomy and modern physics. Because its mathematical laws of planetary motion explained things that could be explained in no other way, the Newtonian system eventually superseded the Cartesian system. But the change came slowly, particularly outside Newton's native land of England. Even Newton himself was reluctant to accept the idea of space being a void, for it was not compatible with his own theories about light waves and colors.

Although he discovered more controlling principles of the physical universe than any man before him, Newton felt deeply frustrated by his inability to find a single pattern that offered answers for everything. "To myself," he admitted, "I seem to have been only like a boy playing on the seashore, and diverting myself in now and then finding a smoother pebble or a prettier shell than ordinary, whilst the great ocean of truth lay all undiscovered before me."

Others rated Newton far more highly than this. In his later life, and especially in the years immediately following his death, he was venerated as the greatest scientist the world had yet known. He proved that the movement of heavenly bodies was governed by exact, changeless laws. He restored people's faith in a universe ruled by order, order no less immutable than that of the revolving Aristotelian spheres. The concept of extrasolar worlds revealing God's glory was therefore closely associated with his name. Before that happened, however, people were convinced by the Cartesians that such worlds did exist.

*

The books of Descartes and Newton, like those of great scientists today, were technical ones full of mathematics. In addition, some were written in Latin, for scholars of of that time still used Latin when they wished to be understood by colleagues in many countries. Ordinary people did not read such books any more than they would now read Einstein's presentation of the theory of relativity. The controversies about cosmology had little effect on the average man, and still less on the average woman, since it was not the custom for women to study philosophy and science. But in 1686 a book appeared that was, in its own way, an even more influential one than Newton's. This book, which has been called the first "popular science" book ever written, was the work of a Frenchman, Bernard de Fontenelle, and its title was *Conversations on the Plurality of Worlds.*

There had been other books on the new astronomy for laymen, but Fontenelle's was vastly more entertaining. It was meant not only for students and literary men, but for people in high society. In France, noblewomen did discuss science with gentlemen at social gatherings. The book took the form of conversations between two lovers: a Marquise—or Countess—and a Parisian philosopher with whom she was strolling through a French garden by starlight. Romance was a courtly, formal affair in seventeenth-century France. If readers found amusement in the eagerness of the Countess to learn astronomy, it was due less to the occasion than to the mere fact that she was a lady.

Fashionable ladies of lesser rank were not amused; they were entranced. In England especially, the Countess became their ideal. Within two years after its publication the book had been translated twice into English, one translation being by a woman, and there were many later editions as well as translations into various European languages. It remained a best-seller until well into the eighteenth century, despite the fact that it was based on the outdated vortex theory of Descartes.

The quotations that follow (including the spelling and punctuation) are taken from a translation made by John Glanvill in 1688. This was the form in which most English-speaking people first became familiar with the idea of inhabited planets outside our solar system:

> The Countess was very impatient to know what would become of the fix'd Stars; are they inhabited, *says she,* as the Planets are, or are they not inhabited? What shall we do with 'em? You may soon guess, *said I;* the fix'd Stars cannot be less distant from the Earth than fifty millions of leagues; nay, if you anger an Astronomer, he will set 'em further. . . . In a word, all the fix'd Stars are so many Suns.

> I perceive, *says the Countess,* where you would carry me; you are going to tell me, that if the fix'd Stars are so many Suns, and our Sun the centre of a Vortex that turns round him, why may not every fix'd Star be the centre of a Vortex that turns round the fix'd Star? Our Sun enlightens the Planets; why may not every fix'd Star have Planets to which they give light? You have said it, *I reply'd,* and I will not contradict you.

> You have made the Universe so large, *says she,* that I know not where I am, or what will become of me; what is it

43

all to be divided into heaps confusedly, one among another? Is every Star the centre of a Vortex, as big as ours? . . . I protest it is dreadful. Dreadful, Madam, *said I;* I think it very pleasant, when the Heavens were a little blue Arch, stuck with Stars, methought the Universe was too strait and close, I was almost stifled for want of Air. . . .

You present me with a kind of Perspective of so vast a length, *said the Countess,* that no Eye can reach to the end of it. . . . The Inhabitants of the Planets which are in other Vortex's . . . are sunk into so great a depth, that tho' I do all I can to see them, yet I must confess I can hardly perceive 'em. . . . We scarce know where we are in the midst of so many Worlds; for my own part, I begin to see the Earth so fearfully little, that I believe from henceforth, I shall never be concern'd at all for any thing: That we so eagerly desire to make ourselves great, that we are always designing, always troubling & harassing our selves, is certainly because we are ignorant of what these Vortex's are.

The Countess and her philosopher did not neglect to speak of love occasionally in the midst of their scientific discussion. Fontenelle managed to use arguments that he felt would be meaningful to ladies who, presumably, had little experience with the reasoning of scholars. Thus when the Countess inquired as to whether it was an absolute necessity that every star have planets, she was answered as follows:

Madam, *said I,* since we are in the humour of mingling amorous Follies with our most serious Discourses, I must tell you, that in Love and the Mathematicks People reason alike: Allow never so little to a Lover, yet presently after you must grant him more; nay more and more, which will at last go a great way: In like manner, grant but a Mathematician one little Principle, he immediately draws a consequence from it, to which you must necessarily assent. . . . These two sorts of People, Lovers and Mathematicians, will always take more than you give 'em. . . .

Now this way of arguing have I made use of. The Moon, *say I,* is inhabited, because she is like the Earth; and the other planets are inhabited, because they are like the Moon; I find the fix'd Stars to be like our Sun, therefore I attribute to them what is proper to that: You are now gone too far to be able to retreat, therefore you must go forward with a good grace.

Reasoning like this, based on extending analogies, was the chief foundation for scientific ideas about other solar systems. Even the belief that their purpose must be habitation arose from the conviction that habitation was the purpose of the earth. As Fontenelle phrased it, "You grant that when two things are like one another in all those things that appear to you, it is possible they may be like one another in those things that are not visible, if you have not some good reason to believe otherwise."

At the time Fontenelle wrote, scientists had no reason to believe that not all planets were alike. There had not been much serious speculation about the nature of other worlds' inhabitants, or about possible differences in their environments. His philosopher did tell the Countess, "So near together are the Vortex's of the Milky way, that the People in one World may talk and shake hands with those of another; at least I believe the Birds of one World may easily fly into another; and that Pigeons may be train'd up to carry Letters." He also suggested that on these worlds so many nearby suns would be visible that there would be no night. However, more prudently than many later writers, he concluded his remarks with, "I think I have said enough for a Man that was never out of his own Vortex."

chapter three

We may pronounce each orb sustains a race
Of living things, adapted to the place. . . .
Were all the stars, whose beauteous realms of light,
At distance only hung to shine by night,
And with their twinkling beams to please our sight?
How many roll in ether, which the eye
Could ne'er, till aided by the glass, descry;
And which no commerce with the Earth maintain!
Are all those glorious empires made in vain?

—Sir Richard Blackmore
Creation (1712)

The first full-length scientific book about life on other planets appeared in 1698 in both Latin and English editions. It was by the Dutch astronomer and physicist Christian Huygens, originator of the wave theory of light, who had died several years earlier. Its title was *The Celestial Worlds Discover'd: or, Conjectures Concerning the Inhabitants, Plants and Productions of the Worlds in the Planets*—and Huygens did include many detailed conjectures. His line of reasoning was in many respects not unlike that employed by modern scientists.

Christian Huygens did not really know anything about life on other planets, of course. Yet like the other eminent scientist of his time, he believed in it. He based his conjectures on sound reasoning, not mere fantasy, although he lacked data for drawing valid conclusions. Certainly his opinions were sincere ones. He was well aware that some readers of his book would "laugh at it as a whimsical and ridiculous undertaking,'' and began by defending his ideas against objections he knew might arise:

> Since then the greatest part of God's creation, that innumerable multitude of Stars, is plac'd out of the reach of any man's Eye; and many of them, it's likely, out of the best Glasses, so that they don't seem to belong to us; is it such an unreasonable Opinion, that there are some reasonable Creatures who see and admire those glorious Bodies at a nearer distance?
>
> But perhaps they'll say, it does not become us to be so curious and inquisitive in these things which the Supreme Creator seems to have kept for his own knowledge. . . . But these Gentlemen must be told, that they take too much upon themselves when they pretend to appoint how far and no farther Men shall go in their Searches, and to set bounds to other Mens Industry; just as if they had been of the Privy Council of Heaven. . . . If our Forefathers had been at this rate scrupulous, we might have been ignorant still of the Magnitude and Figure of the Earth, or of such a place as America. . . .
>
> We shall be less apt to admire what this World calls great, shall nobly despise those Trifles the generality of Men set their affections on, when we know that there are a multitude of such Earths inhabited and adorned as well as our own.

This last argument was frequently used to support the study of other solar systems; indeed it is still being used by thoughtful people today. Very early it was realized that many of the things people care about—and even fight about—would seem quite trivial if viewed from a perspective that included the countless worlds of the universe.

Huygens departed from the common argument that uninhabited worlds would have been made ''in vain, without any design or end,'' for he felt no one could tell why they were made. Nevertheless he was convinced that no planets were without inhabitants: "Not Men perhaps like ours, but some Creatures or other endued with Reason." Otherwise, he said, "Our Earth would have too much advantage of them, in being the only part of the Universe that could boast of such a Creature so far above, not only Plants and Trees, but all Animals whatsoever." For those who might consider mankind nothing to boast about, he added:

> Nor let any one say here, that there's so much Villany and Wickedness in this Man that we have thus magnified, that it's a reasonable doubt, whether he would not be so far from being the Glory and Ornament of the Planet that enjoys his Company, that he would be rather its Shame and Disgrace. . . . The Vices of Men themselves are of excellent use, and are not permitted and allow'd in the World without design. . . .
>
> We must not think that those different Opinions, and that various multiplicity of Minds were place'd in different Men to no end or purpose: but that this mixture of bad Men with good, and the Consequences of such a mixture, as Misfortunes, Wars, Afflictions, Poverty, and the like, were given us for this very good end, *viz.* the exercising of our Wits, and sharpening our Inventions. . . . And if Men were to lead their whole Lives in an undisturb'd continual Peace, in no fear of Poverty, no danger of War, I don't doubt they would live little better than Brutes.

Progress has been made since those words were written, and it is to be hoped that fear of poverty and war can be eliminated; but it could not be eliminated at the time of Huygens. That it led to "sharpening our inventions" is a fact, and one such invention was a means of interplanetary travel. Some people today feel that man might very well be the shame and disgrace of any "planet that enjoys his company," while others feel that expansion to uninhabited planets—those that otherwise seem to exist in vain—will eventually prove to be the best means of getting rid of poverty and war. In either case, it cannot be said that the thoughts of 1698 are irrelevant to the problems of our time.

Going on to discuss the nature of other worlds' inhabitants, Huygens presented long and detailed arguments for their having minds, knowledge and customs similar to ours. He also argued that their bodies must be in some ways similar. For example, he pointed out that hands are so useful that "the Gentlemen that live there must have Hands, or somewhat equally convenient, which is no easy matter; or else we must say that Nature has been kinder not only to us, but even to Squirrels and Monkeys than them." He did not, however, feel that they must necessarily look just like us.

"There is a sort of Animals in the World, as Oysters, Lobsters and Crab-fish, whose Flesh is on the inside of their Bones as 'twere," Huygens wrote. "What if the Planetarians should be such? O no, some body will say, it would be a hideous sight, so ugly, that Nature has not made any but her refuse and meaner Creatures of such an odd Composition. As for that, I should not be at all moved with their ugly shape, if it were not that hereby they would be deprived of that quick easy motion of their Hands. . . . For 'tis a very ridiculous opinion, that the common people have got among them, that it is impossible a rational Soul should dwell in any other shape than ours."

Huygens did not assume, as most other speculators did, that inhabitants of other worlds would be superior to man. He considered the question of whether there might be several rational species on a single planet, but decided that if there were, one must be above the others: "For otherwise, were many endued with the same Wisdom and Cunning, we should have them always doing mischief, always quarreling and fighting one another for Empire and Sovereignty, a thing that we feel too much of where we have but one such Creature." Although he also gave thought to the possibility of their being "so just and good as to be at perpetual Peace," he concluded that "it's more likely they have such a medly as we, such a mixture of good with bad. . . . If there were no other, 'twould be reason enough that we are as good Men as themselves."

Most of Huygens' conjectures applied to the planets of our own solar system, but he considered them applicable to extrasolar planets also. He made this very plain:

Let us fancy our selves placed at an equal distance from the Sun and fix'd Stars; we should then perceive no difference between them. . . . Why then shall not we make use of the same Judgement that we would in that case; and conclude that our Star has no better attendance than the others? So that what we allow'd the Planets, upon the account of our enjoying it, we must likewise grant to all those Planets that surround that prodigious number of Suns. They must have their Plants and Animals, nay and their rational ones too. . . . What a wonderful and amazing Scheme have we here of the magnificent Vastness of the Universe! So many Suns, so many Earths, and every one of them flock'd with so many Herbs, Trees and Animals, and adorned with so many Seas and Mountains!

It must be remembered that Christian Huygens was not an author of fiction, nor was he merely a visionary; he was one of the most distinguished scientists of his age. Today's encyclopedias tell of his achievements in physics and astronomy: not only those connected with the theory of light, but formulation of mathematical theorems that aided Newton's work, invention of the pendulum clock, and discovery of the rings of Saturn. His knowledge of cosmology was incomplete, but his speculations were more objective than most. For instance, about the habitation of the sun, he said, "That the Sun is extremely hot and firy, is beyond all dispute, and such Bodies as ours could not live in such a Furnace. We must make a new sort of Animals then, such as we have no Idea or Likeness of among us, such as we can neither imagine nor conceive: which is as much as to say, that truly we have nothing at all to say."

Both before and after Huygens, there were a great many philosophers and scientists who were unwilling to admit that they had nothing at all to say on such topics. Yet he, despite beliefs about nearby planets that now seem naive, readily drew the line when his lack of data was evident to him. Concerning the number of extrasolar worlds he wrote:

Some of the Antients, and *Jordanus Brunus,* carry'd it further, in declaring the Number infinite: he would persuade us that he has prov'd it by many Arguments, tho in my opinion they are none of them conclusive. Not that I think the contrary can ever be made out. Indeed it seems to me certain, that the Universe is infinitely extended; but what God has bin pleas'd to place beyond the Region of the Stars, is as much above our Knowledge, as it is our Habitation.

*

During the late seventeenth century and early eighteenth century, educated people gave more and more thought to the inhabitants of extrasolar worlds. New ideas about the universe were mingling with old ones. Science of all types seemed to conflict with certain religious beliefs, and men of faith—whether scientists, authors, or clergymen—were anxious to prove that no real conflict existed.

There were two main views of the issue. Some people felt that observation of the universe yielded more religious truth than the Bible did. They did not accept everything the churches taught, and some were not church members at all. Nevertheless, they looked upon astronomy as a subject related to their personal religious beliefs. Many considered it the strongest proof of those beliefs, and wrote a great deal about ''natural theology,'' which meant the study of God as revealed in nature instead of in scripture. The part of nature that seemed most revealing to them was the distant, mysterious part: the region filled with other suns and unknown planets.

On the other hand, there were people who held the Bible to be authoritative and devoted their efforts to reconciling the new astronomy with what it said. In the Bible, they found passages that they interpreted as statements about life beyond Earth. Words that had once been thought to apply to heaven were applied to the newly discovered physical heavens. This was quite logical, since the heaven of religion had formerly been considered a physical realm as well as a spiritual one. But it led to beliefs about other planets' inhabitants that most people of today find strange. Frequently, for instance, the other worlds were assumed to be the homes of the angels.

In a book called *The Sacred Theory of the Earth,* a man named Thomas Burnet mentioned ideas about other worlds that remained current for two hundred years or more. One was the usual argument for their habitation: quoting the Bible, he said, *"God himself that formed the Earth, he created it not in vain, he formed it to be inhabited."* And he continued:

This is true, both of the present Earth and the Future, and of every habitable World whatsoever. For to what purpose is it made habitable, if not to be inhabited? . . . We do not build houses that they should stand empty, but look out for Tenants as fast as we can.

That was something people agreed on whether they cared what the Bible said or not. But Burnet also had more original thoughts. He wrote, "No doubt there are Fixt Stars single, or that have no planets about them . . . nay , 'tis probable, that at first the whole Universe consisted only of such; Globes of liquid Fire, with Spheres about them of pure light and Aether: Earths are but the dirt and skum of the Creation, and all things were pure as they came at first out of the hands of God. But because we have nothing particular taught us, either by the light of Nature or Revelation . . . we leave these Heavenly Systems to the enjoyment and contemplation of higher and more noble Creatures."

This hypothesis about stars, was new to people of Burnet's era, who thought all heavenly bodies had been created at once. Burnet based it on the old notion that the earth was corrupt in comparison to celestial elements; he called planetary systems "last and lowest." It was also connected to a widespread belief that the earth was slowly but surely decaying. Mountains, for example, were usually considered deformities in the seventeenth century, since purity was associated with smooth, perfect spheres.

Because the majority opinion was that all worlds were similar to ours, the distinction Burnet made between habitable and uninhabitable ones was scarcely noticed, and he got no credit for it either from later scientists or from most historians. Some of his other ideas soon became conventional. They too were mixtures of old and new concepts, and the new seemed incontestable when blended with the old. Chief among such ideas was the assumption that extraterrestrial beings were superior to man.

"We must not by any means admit or imagine," wrote Burnet, "that all Nature, and this great Universe, was made only for the sake of Man, the meanest of all Intelligent Creatures that we know of." It may seem odd that he called man "meanest"—that is, least intelligent—since no species higher than man is yet known. But it is understandable in the light of medieval ideas about angels. For hundreds of years people had felt that they knew a great deal about angels; in theology, literature and art there was a long tradition of classifying them into groups of various ranks. When scientific knowledge no longer permitted a literal belief in the traditional angelic regions, it is not surprising that they were transferred to the realm of other planets.

"We have no reason to believe but that there are, at least, as many orders of Beings above us, as there are ranks of Creatures below us," Burnet wrote. "There is a greater distance sure betwixt us and God Almighty, than there is betwixt us and the meanest Worm: and yet we should take it very ill, if the Worms of the Earth should pretend that we were made for them."

This reflects one of the major underlying ideas of European thought: an idea known as the "Great Chain of Being." For a very long period it was believed that there was a strict ladder of rank among the "creatures"—that is, the creations—of God, and that man's rank was in the middle. The animals were below him; the angels or extraterrestrial beings were above him. Every step on the ladder was assumed to be filled. Nothing was known of evolution, so there was no question of a species' moving up a step. And it seemed self-evident that there must be many degrees of superiority among higher beings.

Unlike most, Burnet believed there were also many worlds inhabited by beings more or less equal to man. He said, "If instead of crossing the Seas, we could waft our selves over to our

53

neighbouring Planets, we should meet with such varieties there, both in Nature and Mankind, as would very much enlarge our thoughts and Souls.'' In the case of superior beings, he imagined the old kind of heaven existing within the framework of the new astronomy. Medieval men had not thought of space as dark; they had considered night a shadow cast by the earth. Burnet, too, declared that ''those vast spaces that lie beyond these opake Bodies are Regions of perpetual light.'' Not knowing that space is unlike air, he explained:

> One Hemisphere of a Planet to the other Hemisphere makes night and darkness, but nothing can eclipse the Sun, or intercept the course of his light to these remote Aetherial Regions. They are always luminous, and always pure and serene. And if the worst and Planetary parts of his Dominions be replenisht with Inhabitants, we cannot suppose the better to lie as Desarts, uninjoy'd. . . .
>
> This system of a Fixt Star, with its Planets (of which kind we may imagine innumerable in the Universe, besides this of the Sun, which is near and visible to us) is of a noble Character and Order, being the habitation of Angels and glorified Spirits, as well as of mortal Men.

Not long ago many people would have laughed at the ideas of Thomas Burnet and his contemporaries. Today it is unwise to laugh. The conviction that the earth was decaying (which included an assumption that history would soon end) has its counterpart in modern concern about pollution. The question as to why a world is made habitable, if not to be inhabited, is being asked by many who feel that the ultimate answer to pollution and resource depletion lies in the colonization of uninhabited planets. At the beginning of this century the Russian scientist Konstantin Tsiolkovsky wrote about colonizing space itself, describing it as vast and free and full of light; his dreams of life in orbiting stations are no longer fantastic. And as for the Great Chain of Being, scientists today think it probable that the universe is indeed inhabited by races in varying degrees superior to man.

54

Those who define superiority in moral as well as technological terms speak of qualities formerly used only to describe angels. Hypotheses change, but the truth itself does not change. Perhaps men of past ages saw more of the truth than has been supposed.

*

Not all speculation on astronomy by seventeenth-century religious leaders was based on outdated hypotheses. On December 5th, 1692, a sermon was preached by a young English clergyman, Richard Bentley, who later became a famous scholar. This particular sermon was the last in a series that is well-known because he corresponded with Sir Isaac Newton about it.

Newton's belief in extrasolar planets was strong. He did not write much about such worlds, but in his book *Opticks* he said, "Since space is divisible *in infinitum,* and Matter is not necessarily in all places, it may be also allowed that God is able to create Particles of Matter of several sizes . . . and make Worlds of several sorts in several Parts of the Universe." In an unpublished manuscript quoted by a nineteenth-century biographer he was more specific. There he said, "For in God's house (which is the universe) are many mansions, and he governs them by agents which can pass through the heavens from one mansion to another. For if all places to which we have access are filled with living creatures, why should all these immense spaces of the heavens above the clouds be incapable of inhabitants?"

By "agents which can pass through the heavens" Newton must have meant angels. He made a definite distinction between angels and the inhabitants of the planets, and so did Dr. Bentley. Bentley referred to the latter as "planetary people." His comments about these planetary people began with his conviction that the remote heavenly bodies were not formed merely "to be peeped at through an optic glass." He continued:

Who will deny but that there are great multitudes of lucid stars even beyond the reach of the best telescopes; and that every visible star may have opaque planets revolve about them, which we cannot discover? Now, if they were not created for our sakes, it is certain and evident that they were not made for their own. . . .

It remains, therefore, that all bodies were formed for the sake of intelligent minds. . . each for their own inhabitants which have life and understanding. If any man will indulge himself in this speculation, he need not quarrel with revealed religion upon such an account. The holy Scriptures do not forbid him to suppose as great a multitude of systems, and as much inhabited, as he pleases. . . . Neither need we be solicitous about the condition of those planetary people, nor raise frivolous disputes, how far they participate in the miseries of Adam's fall. . . .

This is exactly what many present-day church leaders have said in the past few decades. But the basic question Richard Bentley discussed was, and still is, of concern to non-Christians as well as to Christians. What he was really talking about was whether or not the inhabitants of other solar systems should be considered human.

The definition of "human" has been debatable ever since the idea of intelligent extraterrestrial life was first conceived. Dr. Bentley's discussion of it was one of the earliest.

What is a man? not a reasonable animal merely, for that is not an adequate and distinguishing definition. . . . A mind of superior or meaner capacities than human would constitute a different species, though united to a human body in the same laws of connexion; and a mind of human capacities would make another species, if united to a different body in different laws of connexion. . . . So that we ought not upon any account to conclude, that if there be rational inhabitants in the moon or Mars, or any unknown planets of other systems, they must therefore have human nature, or be involved in the circumstances of our world.

Some years after Dr. Bentley's sermons, another well-known series was presented by a clergyman named William Derham. He too dealt with nature, but he did not say as much about astronomy as the public wanted to hear. Afterward, therefore, he wrote an entire book entitled *Astro-Theology,* which was first published in 1715 and was extremely popular. William Derham was evidently an amateur astronomer who had studied the subject thoroughly. He was one of the few writers to make an accurate distinction between the original Copernican hypothesis, which "supposeth the firmament of the fixt stars to be the bounds of the universe, and to be placed at equal distance from its center the Sun," and what he called the "new system." The latter, he said, "supposeth there are many other systems of Suns and planets, besides that in which we have our residence: namely, that every fixt star is a Sun, and encompassed with a system of planets."

Possibly it was from books like Dr. Derham's that the idea of people considering the center of the universe the best place was obtained by later writers. Describing one of his diagrams, Derham said, "The Solar system is set in the center of the universe, and figured as a more grand and magnificent part thereof. And so it may be looked upon by us, by reason of its proximity and relation to us. But whether it be really so, whether it be in the center of the universe, and whether, among all the noble train of fixt stars, there be no system exceeding ours in its magnificent retinue of planets . . . is a difficulty out of the reach of our glasses."

By this, he meant that he had necessarily drawn our solar system in the center of the diagram and made it look more grand and magnificent than all the stars he drew around the edge, "for want of room to lay out all the several systems in due proportion." Moreover, he was speaking not of the *earth,* but of the *whole solar system,* when he suggested that central position might give an impression of magnificence. Readers of Derham's era were familiar with books such as Bishop Wilkins', which referred to the old Aristotelian idea that the least perfect body must be in the center; but many later ones were not.

Dr. Derham, like most of his educated contemporaries, believed that "As myriads of systems are more for the glory of God . . . than one, so it is no less probable than possible, there may be many besides this which we have the privilege of living in." He too declared that planets would be of no use if not inhabited, but he made no guesses about what the inhabitants were like. The reader who was interested, he suggested, might "find a pleasant entertainment in the great Mr. Christian Huygens's Cosmotheros. . . . To which I shall refer him, rather than give either him or myself any farther trouble about these matters, which are merely conjectural."

Most of *Astro-Theology* was devoted to long descriptions of the vastness of the universe, and of the order in it shown by the arrangement and movement of planets. Dr. Derham wondered that there could be "any found, among rational Beings, so stupid, so vile, so infatuated with their own vices, as to deny these works to be God's, and ascribe them to a necessity of nature, or indeed a mere nothing, namely, chance!" In part, this was an attempt to make plain that belief in many worlds did not mean agreement with the other ideas of the ancient Greek philosopher Democritus, who had indeed believed that worlds were created by chance; ever since medieval times association with Democritus had been a serious handicap to the whole plurality of worlds concept. But the vehemence of William Derham's attack shows that people of his own time were beginning to interpret scientific discoveries in a more modern way. They were speculating not only about chance, but about "necessity of nature."

At the very end of *Astro-Theology,* William Derham wrote of an idea that seems to have been widespread in eighteenth-century England, and that frequently appeared in poetry of the era:

> We are naturally pleased with new things; we take great pains, undergo dangerous voyages, to view other countries: with great delight we hear of new discoveries in the Heavens, and view those glorious bodies with great pleasure thro' our glasses. With what pleasure then shall happy departed souls survey the most distant regions of the universe, and view all those glorious globes thereof, and their noble appendages with a nearer view?

That departed souls visit other planets after death is not a traditional doctrine of the Christian religion, but it is easy to see why it appealed to people. So much was being said about all the glorious worlds of the universe that the thought of never seeing them had become, to the enthusiasts, nearly unbearable.

*

Enthusiasm for other worlds was by no means limited to scientists and clergymen in eighteenth-century England. For several decades it was so strong among laymen that it might almost be called a fad. The interest of women aroused by Fontenelle's book about the Countess grew and grew. Fashionable ladies who could afford them had their own telescopes, and those who could not nevertheless became amateur astronomers to the extent of reading and discussing other books on the subject. One of the best known books was *Newtonianism for Ladies,* a science book translated from Italian by a young Englishwoman who was among the most learned ladies of her time. It has been said that the topic of extrasolar planets may have contributed more than any other to the development of education for women in that period.

To be sure, large numbers of eighteenth-century people did not have much education. Schooling was not free, and few working men could obtain it for themselves, much less for their daughters. They did not read the things popular in literary circles or attend lectures where such ideas were discussed. Therefore, it cannot be said that the majority of the population either knew or cared about astronomy. However, among educated people, it was unquestionably a major field of interest.

This is shown by the literary newspapers of the era. Probably the most famous paper is *The Spectator*, which contained essays instead of news but was published daily. One of its editors was Joseph Addison. Among many other things, Addison wrote the familiar hymn, "The Spacious Firmament on High," which is sung in many churches today but which first appeared in *The Spectator* on August 23, 1712. Because the hymn does not mention other worlds, it is sometimes thought that phrases such as "Spangled Heav'ns, a Shining Frame" mean that Addison thought in terms of the old cosmology. But only a few weeks earlier, on July 12, he had said in *The Spectator:*

> If we yet rise higher, and consider the fixt Starrs as so many vast Oceans of Flame, that are each of them attended with a different Sett of Planets, and still discover new Firmaments and new Lights, that are sunk farther in those unfathomable depths of Ether, so as not to be seen by the strongest of our Telescopes, we are lost in such a Labyrinth of Suns and Worlds, and confounded with the Immensity and Magnificence of Nature.

These words prove that to Addison the "Shining Frame" did encompass solar systems other than ours. Also, in one *Spectator* issue he remarked that Fontenelle drew a very good argument for "the peopling of every planet." And in another he used the Great Chain of Being concept to argue for the existence of races superior to man. In the paper for July 9, 1714, he wrote:

> When I considered that infinite Hoste of Stars, or, to speak more Philosophically, of Suns, which were then shining upon me, with those innumerable Sets of Planets or Worlds, which were moving round their respective Suns . . . I could not but reflect on that little insignificant Figure which I my self bore amidst the Immensity of God's Works.

Feelings like this did trouble many people, and many overcame them—as Addison did—by the belief that God cared for "every thing that has Being" on all worlds of all solar systems. Then too, some thought it would be a good thing if such feelings were more widespread. George Berkeley, one of the most notable philosophers of the time, wrote in another paper, *The Guardian:* "It were to be wished a certain prince, who hath encouraged the study of it in his subjects, had been himself proficient in astronomy. This might have shown him how mean an ambition . . . terminated in a small part of what is itself but a point in respect of that part of the universe which lies within our view." Berkeley was referring to King Louis XIV of France, who had spent large sums of his people's tax money building a luxurious palace for himself.

Even political leaders were interested enough in planets of other solar systems to write about them. One, Lord Bolingbroke, discussed them in several essays, in one of which he said:

> The planets of our solar system, and the same may be assumed of a multitude of other solar systems which the immensity of the universe contains, are worlds that have an analogy with ours, and the habitations of animals that have an analogy with us. . . . Shall we be so absurd and so impertinent now as to imagine that all these . . . are confined to the same degree of intelligence, or even to the same manner of knowing? Or rather than believe that they are in these, and perhaps other respects, superior to us, shall we assert that there are no such beings, and deny that they exist, though we discover some of their habitations? . . .

> We cannot discern a gradation of beings in other planets by the help of our telescopes . . . but the gradation of sense and intelligence in our own from animal to animal . . . as well as the very abrupt manner, if I may say so, in which this evidently unfinished intellectual system stops at the human species, gives great reason to believe that this gradation is continued upwards in other systems, as we perceive it to be downwards in ours. We may well suspect that ours is the lowest, in this respect, of all mundane systems . . . and there may be as much difference between some other creature of God, without having recourse to angels and archangels, and man, as there is between a man and an oyster.

By far the most frequent mention of extrasolar worlds, at least in eighteenth-century writings that have survived, came in poetry. The poets of the era, both famous ones and those who are not so famous, were enraptured by the idea. At that time poems were frequently many pages long; in fact they sometimes filled whole volumes. The passages of verse at the beginnings of the chapters in this book are merely short excerpts. They represent only a fraction of the pertinent things poets said about other planets and the beings that might inhabit them.

Most of this verse is not considered great poetry today. Yet when it was newer, it was popular and much admired. Of Edward Young's *Night Thoughts* (small portions of which appear on pages 65 and 153 of this book) one nineteenth-century writer said: "Editions have been multiplied from every press in the country. It is to be seen of the shelf of the cottager, with the Family Bible and *Pilgrim's Progress;* and it ranks among the first and favourite materials of the poetical library." This writer also remarked that Napoleon was said to be particularly fond of it.

Night Thoughts was a long book with the entire last section devoted to astronomy. Edward Young found the thought of an immense universe full of worlds exhilarating. He titled the astronomical section "The Consolation" because in the rest of the poem he had dwelt on the gloomier aspects of life, and he really believed that contemplation of the stars was the best consolation for the evils of Earth. "Nothing can satisfy but what confounds," he wrote. The awe and wonder inspired by countless suns supported his faith.

About the inhabitants of those suns' worlds Edward Young wrote a great deal; he alternated between viewing them as angels, and wondering whether they had problems similar to ours. He even phrased sections of the poem as if he were speaking to them. "You never heard of man," he said ruefully. "Or earth, the bedlam of the universe! . . . Has the least rumour of our race arrived?" This emotion was much like that shared by many people today. So was this:

> The soul of man was made to walk the skies;
> Delightful outlet of her prison here!
> There, disincumbered from her chains, the ties
> Of toys terrestrial, she can rove at large. . . .

By the time Edward Young wrote *Night Thoughts*, in 1745, there had already been a great many poems dealing with extrasolar worlds. Even Alexander Pope's well-known *Essay on Man* devoted a few lines to the subject:

> Thro' worlds unnumber'd tho' the God be known,
> 'Tis ours to trace him only in our own.
> He who thro' vast immensity can pierce,
> See worlds on worlds compose one universe,
> Observe how system into system runs,
> What other planets circle other suns,
> What varied being peoples every star,
> May tell why Heav'n has made us as we are.

Those lines are sometimes quoted today as if they were an exceptional case of early interest in other solar systems. Not many people realize that Alexander Pope was criticizing the common practice of his contemporaries. That poetry should concentrate on our own world was a novel suggestion; dozens of minor poets described the ''worlds unnumber'd'' and their inhabitants at tedious length. They also described imaginary cosmic voyages—not voyages in spaceships, but dream trips and journeys of the soul after death.

Poems of this last type were particularly popular following the death of Sir Isaac Newton. Many people could not believe that so great a man as Newton would not have a chance to view suns and their planets at close range before entering heaven. One woman wrote:

> With faculties enlarg'd, he's gone to prove
> The laws and motions of yon worlds above;
> And the vast circuits of th'expanse survey,
> View solar systems in the Milky Way.

This example is typical of feelings widespread in that age, when people were beginning to discover the limitations of science. In the old days, they had been content with the closed Aristotelian universe and had not aspired to see beyond its bounds. That was no longer true. Some were satisfied to merely read about distant worlds, but others had become a bit wistful; imaginary accounts were not enough for them. The idea of space travel as a potential reality had not yet occurred to anybody, for the brief comments of Kepler and Bishop Wilkins had not been taken seriously. More in keeping with the hopes of the era were words like these—from Robert Gambol's *Beauties of the Universe*—that told of a time when the soul

> Unbounded in its ken, from prison free
> Will clearly view what here we darkly see:
> Those planetary worlds, and thousands more,
> Now veil'd from human sight, it shall explore.

The spiritual concept of heaven was still blended with the physical one. The two had been separated by scientists, but not yet by poets or the general public. Today, people who believe in a life after death do not usually envision it as a means of seeing faraway planets. The hope of seeing them has found other channels of expression; it has become a hope for mankind's future instead of for one's personal future. Yet the longing to know more of those worlds has remained the same.

chapter four

Is not this home creation, in the map
Of universal nature, as a speck,
Like fair Britannia in our little ball;
Exceeding fair, and glorious for its size,
But, elsewhere, far outmeasured, far outshone?
In fancy (for the fact beyond us lies,)
Canst thou not figure it, an isle, almost
Too small for notice, in the vast of being;
Severed by mighty seas of unbuilt space
From other realms; from ample continents
Of higher life, where nobler natives dwell?

—Edward Young
Night Thoughts (1745)

By the middle of the eighteenth century, plurality of worlds was no longer a fad among educated people; the most fashionable enthusiams were for other things. But the belief in extrasolar planets had become a basic one that was to endure unchanged for more than a hundred years.

One proof that this belief was well established is the mention of it in books for children. Adults do not buy nonfiction books for children unless they consider them factual, so the successful ones must have been approved by most authorities. Such a book was published by John Newbery, the first well-known publisher of children's books in England. In 1758 he brought out a book entitled *The Newtonian System of Philosophy Adapted to the Capacities of Young Gentlemen and Ladies . . . Being the Substance of Six Lectures read to the Lilliputian Society, by Tom*

Telescope, and Collected . . . by their Old Friend Mr. Newbery in St. Paul's Church-Yard. . . . "Tom Telescope" was, of course, a fictional character, and scholars believe the book was probably written by John Newbery himself. It was a best-seller and had many later editions. The following statement comes from an edition of 1812:

Some philosophers have concluded, and I think not without reason, that every fixed star is a sun that has a system of planets revolving round it, like our solar system. And if so, how immensely great, how wonderfully glorious is the structure of this universe, which contains many thousand worlds as large as ours, suspended in aether, rolling like the earth round their several suns, and filled with animals, plants, and minerals, all perhaps different from ours, but all intended to magnify the Almighty Architect.

Like Fontenelle's *Plurality of Worlds* and other popular science books of the time, Newbery's was written in the form of dialogue between imaginary people, interspersed with narrative—in this case, between Tom Telescope and a group of children. After Tom Telescope's speech quoted above, "The fervor and air of piety with which this was delivered silenced every disposition to levity and ridicule. . . . Master Wilson, who had before been very impertinent, began now to feel abashed." Books written in the eighteenth century lost no opportunity to bring in a moral.

Another book for children that had many editions was *Easy Introduction to Astronomy for Young Gentlemen and Ladies,* by James Ferguson, who also wrote one of the best-known astronomy books for adults. The *Easy Introduction* was first published in 1768, in London, but the quotations here are from a Philadelphia edition of 1819. In this book the conversations were between a brother and sister. The girl, Eudosia, wanted her brother—who had just come home from college—to teach her something about "the sublime science of Astronomy," but she was a little afraid to ask him. "Perhaps you may think me too vain," she ventured, "in wanting to know what the bulk of mankind think our sex have no business with. . . . Shall I not be laughed at for attempting to learn what men say is fit only for *men* to know?"

"Never by any man who thinks right," her brother assured her, "and I hope you are above minding what those say who think wrong." After he had told her a great many technical details about astronomy, such as how to predict eclipses, they discussed inhabitants of other worlds.

At first Eudosia was troubled by the thought of some planets receiving more light than others, for she did not believe God would be partial. "I cannot imagine the inhabitants of our earth to be better than those of other planets," she protested. "On the contrary, I would fain hope they have not acted so absurdly, with respect to him, as we have done." Her brother then explained that the eyes of different planets' people would be adapted to the amount of sunlight each planet received. This was in reference to the planets of our own solar system. When he began to speak of others, Eudosia was astonished, and exclaimed, "What! other suns, and planetary worlds belonging to them! You amaze me!"

Familiar as the idea was to people with knowledge of astronomy, the majority had no such knowledge. And girls still had little opportunity to study science at all; Eudosia sighed "because there is not an university for ladies as well as for gentlemen." In 1768, when Ferguson wrote, such developments were yet to come.

His book continued to sell during the early nineteenth century, but by then more up-to-date ones existed also: for example, *Young Ladies' Astronomy . . . Designed Particularly for the Assistance of Young Ladies in that Interesting and Sublime Study, though Well Adapted to the Use of Common Schools,* published in 1825. That one had a question-and-answer format:

For what purpose are these multiplied systems of worlds supposed to have been created?

They are supposed to have been designed for the abode of animal life; and if so, they are probably inhabited, at this

moment, by an innumerable number of accountable beings.
. . .

What reason have we to warrant the supposition that all the worlds which astronomy contemplates are inhabited?

From what is known respecting our own system . . . we infer that all the other systems are similarly constructed and adapted to the support of human creatures, and that they of course are really inhabited. . . .

But will not the conclusion militate against the acknowledged truths of the Bible?

. . . That sacred volume, it is true, does not expressly admit of a plurality of worlds, nor does it any where deny their existence; we cannot thence conclude that they do not exist. . . .

What would be the tendency of a total rejection of a plurality of worlds?

The tendency would be to discredit a system harmonizing and beautiful in all its parts. . . The tendency would also be to narrow our conceptions of God's character, and to rob him of some of those exalted attributes assigned him by the unlettered savage.

Today, most science books do not mention the Bible, since people's religious beliefs are kept separate from information about science. That was not the case in past centuries. Though there were people then who did not feel that the Bible had any bearing on the matter, just as there are now, they did not think it strange for an astronomy book to point out that nothing in the Bible prevented those who considered it an authority from believing in such worlds. The book was not connected with any church. Nor was it one that appealed only to space enthusiasts. It was a recommended text for the "common schools," and its preface included an endorsement signed by the Governor of the State of New York, who stated that he had read most of the proof-sheets.

Another kind of evidence for widespread belief in extrasolar worlds during the eighteenth and nineteenth centuries comes from casual statements made by famous men of that time whose main interests were in other fields. These statements are hard to locate; they are rarely mentioned by historians and most can therefore be found only in complete sets of such men's works. Nevertheless, many exist, of which the following are typical examples.

Quite a few notable men of colonial America referred to the belief. For instance, a book called *The Christian Philosopher* was written by the Puritan minister Cotton Mather, who is most famous today for his involvement in the Salem witchcraft trials. He was not the sort of man who would be expected to have much interest in extrasolar planets. Yet his book devoted many pages to the subject. Unlike most, Cotton Mather did not claim to know the purpose of other planets, though he assumed they were inhabited. He wrote:

> Great GOD, what a Variety of Worlds hast thou created! How astonishing are the Dimensions of them! How stupendous are the Displays of thy Greatness, and of thy Glory, in the Creatures with which thou hast replenished those Worlds! . . . Who can tell what Uses those marvellous Globes may be designed for.

Benjamin Franklin was also a firm believer both in other solar systems and in the superiority of their inhabitants to man. In 1728 he wrote:

> I believe that Man is not the most perfect Being but One, rather that as there are many Degrees of Beings his Inferiors, so there are many Degrees of Beings superior to him.
>
> Also, when I stretch my Imagination thro' and beyond our System of Planets, beyond the visible fix'd Stars themselves, into that Space that is every Way infinite, and conceive it fill'd with Suns like ours, each with a Chorus of Worlds for ever moving round him, then this little Ball on

which we move seems, even in my narrow Imagination, to be almost Nothing.

This was part of a statement about his private religious beliefs, in which speculations about other solar systems played a large part. But he mentioned extraterrestrial beings in connection with science, too. In *Poor Richard's Almanac* for September, 1749, Benjamin Franklin wrote, "It is the opinion of all the modern philosophers and mathematicians that the planets are habitable worlds." In the middle of a letter to a friend explaining his own hypothesis about magnetism, he said, "Superior beings smile at our theories, and at our presumption in making them." To another friend he expressed the wish that the friend's idea of happy conduct might "grow and increase till it becomes the governing philosophy of the human species, as it must be that of superior beings in better worlds."

Thomas Jefferson, despite great interest in science, did not say much about extrasolar planets in his writings; but the catalog of his library shows that he owned the books on plurality of worlds by Fontenelle, Huygens, and William Derham. So he must have thought about the subject. Once, in a personal letter, he spoke of the "new scene" presented by the thought of planets orbiting variable stars.

The diary of John Adams, who became the second president of the United States, also contains references to other solar systems. On the 24th of April, 1756, he wrote, "Astonomers tell us, with good Reason, that . . . all the unnumbered Worlds that revolve round the fixt Starrs are inhabited, as well as this Globe of Earth." That day and the next, he went on to reflect upon whether all the "different Ranks of Rational Beings" in those worlds had committed moral wickedness, and if so, whether any church leaders would think they must be "consigned to everlasting Perdition." It is evident that he himself did not think so.

Some people of today find it surprising that everyone who considered extrasolar worlds in past centuries immediately connected the subject with religion. After all, many were not especially religious in everyday life. John Adams, for example, was mainly concerned with law, politics and government; he devoted most of his time and attention to those affairs. Certainly plenty of men thought about religion only on Sunday, and not even then if they were not church-goers.

Religion, however, is not merely what is believed by those who belong to some specific group with specific traditions. In its broad sense, it is a way of interpreting the mysteries of the universe. One modern dictionary lists "concern over what exists beyond the visible world" as its first definition of the word. Until the twentieth century, it did not occur to anyone that science could find out anything about worlds of other suns. Science knew that stars *were* suns, and that was all. So scientists, politicians, and everybody else assumed that ideas concerning distant solar systems were religious ideas. They did not all associate those ideas with the official views of any church, but they nevertheless associated them with their own religious views. There was no other category in which to put them.

The author Philip Freneau is known chiefly as "the poet of the American Revolution" because that was the subject he wrote most about. But in a poem about nature he spoke of:

> A power, that every blessing gives,
> Who through eternal ages lives,
> All space inhabits, space his throne,
> Spreads through all worlds, confin'd to none.

He and most others who contemplated such a power called it God. Yet even those who did not use that name believed that the many worlds of the universe belonged to a pattern, a pattern science could not describe.

*

Scientists tried to describe the pattern, of course, and with respect to its physical aspects they made progress. Sometimes the progress was initiated by people whose view was not particularly scientific. In 1750 an Englishman, Thomas Wright, published a book called *An Original Theory or New Hypothesis of the Universe*. Though his lengthy arguments for inhabited planets of

71

other suns were common ones, in addition he argued for an idea that was indeed new: the idea that the stars themselves revolved around a central point. He declared that the Milky Way was an orderly system of stars that included our sun. In other words, he introduced the concept of galaxies.

After calculating that there must be "within the whole celestial Area 60,000,000 planetary Worlds like ours," Thomas Wright said:

> In this great Celestial Creation, the Catastrophy of a World such as ours, or even the total Dissolution of a System of Worlds, may possibly be no more to the great Author of Nature, than the most common Accident in Life with us, and in all Probability such final and general Doom-Days may be as frequent there as even Birthdays, or Mortality with us upon the Earth. This Idea has something so cheerful in it, that I own I can never look upon the Stars without wondering why the whole World does not become Astronomers.

This thought does not strike most people as cheerful. But Wright felt that it turned men's attention from "all the Vicissitudes of adverse Fortune, which make so many narrow-minded Mortals miserable." Above all, it made him want to reconcile the spiritual heaven with the physical universe again. He believed heaven was a place equally accessible to souls from the worlds of all suns. It was on that basis, as well as on the basis of analogy between order within solar systems and a larger order of stellar ones, that he developed his idea about the Milky Way. To Wright, the center around which suns moved was "far superior to any other Point of Situation in the known Universe"; unlike earlier thinkers who had assumed a central position to be "low," he envisioned the middle as the throne of God.

Most astronomers had long before abandoned the idea of a physical location for heaven, so Wright's book did not have much influence, despite the fact that his view of the galaxy—and of nebulae as other galaxies—was amazingly correct. However, he was given credit by the first man to present a theory of galaxies in scientific terms.

That man was the German philosopher Immanuel Kant. In his *Universal Natural History and Theory of the Heavens,* written in 1755, Kant observed that scientific cosmology had not changed since the time of Huygens, when, though it was recognized that "infinite space swarms with worlds," the fixed stars "were looked upon as filling all the heavens . . . without order and without intention." He then went on to discuss his theory of the Milky Way, and of the nebulae as similar but vastly more distant star-systems, saying of it:

> With what astonishment are we transported when we behold the infinite multitude of worlds and systems which fill the extension of the Milky Way! But how is this astonishment increased, when we become aware of the fact that all these immense orders of star-worlds again form but one of a number whose termination we do not know. . . . There is here no end but an abyss of a real immensity, in presence of which all the capability of human conception sinks exhausted.

Overwhelming as this enlarged concept of the universe may seem, it was less dismaying to most minds than the presumed lack of order in the stellar regions had been. The thought of there being no center had disturbed people more than the removal of the earth from the center. Kant's theory restored a "universal centre of the attraction of the whole of nature." This led him to another new and significant concept: he believed that the universe was formed from the center outward.

> The sphere of developed nature is incessantly engaged in extending itself. Creation is not the work of a moment. . . . Millions and whole myriads of millions of centuries will flow on, during which always new worlds and new systems of worlds will be formed after each other in the distant regions away from the centre of nature, and will attain to perfection. . . . While nature thus adorns eternity with changing scenes, God continues engaged in incessant

creation in forming the matter for construction of still greater worlds.

Such ideas as these, which Kant elaborated in detail, have much in common with some present-day cosmological theories. Moreover, Kant was ahead of his time in still another way. He did not think *all* planets were necessarily inhabited. That, he felt, "would be as if one were to make the wisdom of God a reason for doubting the fact that sandy deserts occupy wide areas of the earth's surface and that there are islands in the sea without human inhabitants; for a planet is a much smaller thing in comparison with the whole creation than a desert or an island in comparison with the earth's surface." And he also felt that it was likely "that celestial bodies which are not yet inhabited will be hereafter, when their development has reached a later stage."

This farsighted picture of evolving worlds and an evolving universe did not become prevalent until long after Immanuel Kant's time. Moreover, most of what Kant wrote about other worlds' inhabitants was omitted from his book when it was finally translated into English. He believed that peoples of planets far from their suns must be morally superior to those of warmer worlds, an opinion later scientists did not share; perhaps they thought his speculations on such matters unlikely to enhance his reputation as one of the world's greatest philosophers. Kant gained that reputation mainly from what he wrote on topics other than cosmology. Only his hypothesis about the Milky Way and the nebulae was adopted by the astronomers of his era.

Foremost among those astronomers was Sir William Herschel, the first man to study the stars systematically with a telescope. His many achievements, which included the discovery of the planet Uranus, made him well known to the general public. Although his writings were technical ones, published in scientific journals, his discoveries and opinions were widely reported in newspapers and magazines. Everyone who had an interest in astronomy admired Herschel. And Herschel's belief in a multitude of inhabited worlds was even stronger than most people's. Unlike other notable astonomers he was convinced that the moon, and even the sun, were inhabited as well as the planets.

This conviction he naturally applied to other suns also.

Because Sir William Herschel was an observational astronomer instead of a mere speculator, his voice carried great weight—although of course, his thoughts about the inhabitants of planets and suns were as speculative as anybody else's. He did not pretend to have observed any inhabitants. People who were not scientists, however, frequently assumed that he knew more than he had any way of knowing.

Herschel had no means of knowing more about extraterrestrial life than his contemporaries. On the other hand, it should not be thought—as it was by scientists at one time—that his reasoning was less sound than theirs. He was aware that life of the same kind as Earth's could not exist on the sun, although he did think that the interior of the sun was cooler than the luminous exterior. What he believed was that "it is most probably inhabited, like the rest of the planets, by beings whose organs are adapted to the peculiar circumstance of that vast globe." Since the time of Giordano Bruno speculators about life on other worlds have been divided into those who have held that it must be confined to environments similar to ours, and those who have seen no reason to impose such a limitation. From the scientific standpoint, the question is one of biology, not astronomy. Astronomy cannot settle it now any more than it could two hundred years ago, when William Herschel lived.

*

It is difficult to determine whether the idea of countless solar systems was as popular throughout the rest of the world as it was in England and America. Most of the writing about it is in books or magazines now relatively rare, and not of the sort usually translated. One would have to be able to read many languages, and visit large foreign libraries, to find out what the prevailing opinion among educated people in other countries was. The great scientists and philosophers of Western civilization, however, came from many nations, and quoted each other's works; in the eighteenth and nineteenth centuries a number of them referred to the existence of extrasolar planets as undisputed fact. Those who did not seem to have been silent on the subject.

Much less information is available about Eastern civilization. Vedic scriptures spoke of many worlds. So did ancient Buddhist writings, and the thirteenth-century Chinese scholar Tong Mu wrote:

> Empty space is like a kingdom and heaven and earth no more than a single individual person in that kingdom. Upon one tree there are many fruits, and in one kingdom many people. How unreasonable it would be to suppose that besides the heaven and earth which we can see there are no other heavens and no other earths!

In China, people never believed in Aristotelian cosmology with its enclosed system of crystal spheres; throughout medieval times they pictured space as containing other worlds. Western scholars who visited China in the seventeenth century learned this, so European books about plurality of worlds written in that century often mentioned China. But the Chinese then thought of "other worlds" in a general sense rather than of solar systems. English books do not seem to tell when they, or other Eastern peoples, began to believe that planets circled the stars.

Eighteenth-century Russia had close cultural ties with Western Europe, and both Fontenelle's book and Huygens' were translated into Russian. The Russian scientist and poet Mikhail Lomonosov was especially interested in extrasolar life. He mentioned it in one of his best-known poems, "Evening Meditations on Seeing the Aurora Borealis."

> Science tells me that each twinkling star
> That smiles above us is a peopled sphere,
> Or central sun, diffusing light afar;
> A link of nature's chain. . . .
>
> Vain is the inquiry—all is darkness, doubt:
> This earth is one vast mystery to man.
> First find the secrets of this planet out,
> Then other planets, other systems scan!

76

In Sweden, the most famous writer about other worlds was Emanuel Swedenborg, a distinguished scientist who later became a mystic and theologian. His book *The Earths in our Solar System, which are called Planets, and the Earths in the Starry Heaven* was not science, but an account of his mystic experiences. He believed that he had conversed with the spirits of other worlds' inhabitants and had traveled—in a spiritual rather than a bodily sense—to many distant planets. In the book he gave detailed descriptions of them. Swedenborg was a learned man of high reputation, one who had made significant inventions and proposed advanced theories in both physics and physiology. His beliefs were sincere, although the majority of people did not share them, and after he died a church was founded based on his theological writings. One of his principal teachings was that the peoples of all worlds were human.

The conviction that inhabited worlds surround other suns was unquestionably common to men and women of many nationalities and faiths, though a few cautioned against jumping to conclusions for which there was no proof. John Wesley, the founder of the Methodist Church, wrote: "It is our wisdom to be very wary how we pronounce concerning things we have not seen." He said he did not contest the probability of other worlds being inhabited, but insisted—quite rightly—that no real evidence existed. "Be not so *positive*," he continued, "especially with regard to things which are neither easy nor necessary to be determined."

But as a rule, people did not doubt the truth of the predominant view. The president of Yale University, Timothy Dwight, stated unequivocally that the stars "are known with absolute certainty to be universally suns, resembling our own." He went on to declare that systems of planets were "with the highest reason supposed to exist and to be, like the earth, the residence of intelligent beings." When this idea first raised controversy again, the point at issue was not the assumption itself, but its implications. That issue became a heated one in 1794, following the publication of a book called *Age of Reason* by Thomas Paine.

Thomas Paine was one of the foremost patriots of the American Revolution. The things he had written before and during the

Revolution had played a major part in shaping public opinion. He was no scholarly philosopher, writing mainly for an audience of other philosophers. His words were addressed to the general public—and he deliberately made them fervent, even shocking, in order to hold people's attention. His name was well known to everyone. After America won independence, Paine continued to write about politics, and he became involved in the French Revolution, which led to his imprisonment in France.

While he was in prison, Thomas Paine thought he might not get out alive; so, fearing that he would never have another chance, he wrote a book about his religious beliefs. Actually those beliefs were not very different from those of many other educated eighteenth-century men, but such ideas had been expressed in scholarly works rather than popular ones, and had not reached average people. When Paine got out of prison and his book was published, it aroused a storm of protest.

Age of Reason presented to common men what had been discussed in literary and scientific circles for at least a century: the idea that knowledge of God should be sought in nature instead of in supernatural revelation. Many of them were furious. Many churchmen were furious also; though they had been willing to let a minority of philosophers and scientists think that way, they felt the faith of less educated people would be destroyed. In addition, Paine's political enemies, who were anxious to discredit him, falsely accused him of being an atheist. The result of all this was that both the book itself and the angry replies to it were widely circulated. Because Paine had included a long description of a universe full of solar systems to make his point, the concept got more attention than ever before.

In the seventeenth century, statements in the Bible had been used as arguments against the new cosmology; Thomas Paine did the opposite: he used the new cosmology, which was no longer new, as an argument against statements in the Bible. "To believe that God created a plurality of worlds at least as numerous as what we call stars," he wrote, "renders the Christian system of faith at once little and ridiculous, and scatters it in the mind like feathers in the air. The two beliefs cannot be held together in the same mind, and he who thinks he believes both, has thought but little of either.''

That was Thomas Paine's honest opinion, but it was untrue, Many people believed both in plurality of worlds and in Christianity; many still do. Such people had often thought a great deal about it, and had reached conclusions unlike Paine's. He asked, ''From whence, then, could arise the solitary and strange conceit that the Almightly, who had millions of worlds equally dependent on his protection, should quit the care of all the rest, and come to die in our world, because, they say, one man and one woman had eaten an apple? And on the other hand, are we to suppose that every world in the boundless creation had an Eve, an apple, a serpent and a redeemer?''

Besides seeming irreverent to people, this was open to attack on grounds of logic. Paine must have known that some Christians interpreted the story of the apple and the serpent as an allegory, yet the force of his argument depended on taking it literally. A more important logical flaw was that even to those who did take it literally, it was by no means a valid assumption that God abandoned all the other planets for the sake of ours. As one writer put it:

> Mr. Paine seems to wish to have it thought that the doctrine of a multiplicity of inhabited worlds is a matter of *demonstration;* but the existence of a number of heavenly bodies, whose revolutions are under the direction of certain laws . . . does not prove that they are all inhabited by intelligent beings. I do not deny that, from other considerations, the thing may be highly probable; but it is not more than a probability. . . . But I do not wish to avail myself of these observations, as I am under no apprehensions that the cause in which I engage requires them.

This writer's ''cause'' was to point out that plurality of worlds was not necessarily incompatible with Christianity, and a great many others engaged in it during the next few decades. As it happened, what some of them said restored in people's minds the idea that Earth had a central position in the affairs of the universe, spiritually if not physically. Most Christians of that time held either that only on Earth had the inhabitants sinned, using the parable of the Good Shepherd to suggest that God devoted special care to the one world that needed saving, or that Earth had been singled out as the site of events that affected the populations of all the other planets.

In addition, new emphasis was placed on the old idea of the other worlds being inhabited by angels. By no means everyone agreed with it, but it became popular among large groups that had formerly known little if anything about astronomy. The most celebrated presentation of this view was by Thomas Chalmers, whose book—usually known by its abbreviated title of *Astronomical Discourses*—was a best-seller for many years during the nineteenth century. The *British Review* reported that the volume had "suspended for a time every other fashionable topic of the literary kind, and spread as far as any tale of unholy love, mysterious murder, or sentimental crime."

Thomas Chalmers was a Scottish clergyman famed for his preaching ability, and the *Astronomical Discourses* were originally sermons given in Scotland in 1817. Many years later the author of a magazine article wrote: "One or two of these 'Discourses' . . . delivered in the Tron Church, Glasgow, at noon on the week-day, were heard by the writer of this paper, then a boy. He had to wait nearly four hours before he could gain admission as one of a crowd in which he was nearly crushed to death. It was with no little effort that the great preacher could find his way to his pulpit. . . . In that enthusiasm the writer, young as he was, fully participated. He has never since witnessed anything equal to the scene."

Dr. Chalmers presented the case for extrasolar worlds with great eloquence, and from his explanations of astronomy it is evident that his audience included people not already familiar with the subject. Today, his sermons would seem extremely long and repetitive; but so would all sermons of that era—and Dr. Chalmers was a more effective orator than most. He drew a vivid picture of Earth, "one of the smaller islets which float on the ocean of vacancy," as the scene of a contest between angelic hosts and the legions of the devil. "Though we know little or nothing of the moral economy of the other planets," he said, "we are not to infer that the beings who occupy these widely extended regions . . . know little of ours. . . . Angels have a mightier reach of contemplation. Angels can look upon this world, and all which it inherits, as the part of a larger family. Angels were in the full exercise of their powers even at the first infancy of our species . . . they regard us as heirs of the same destiny with themselves, to rise along with them in the scale of moral elevation."

Anyone who is inclined to dismiss this as a totally outmoded way of viewing the universe might find it interesting to compare Dr. Chalmers' ideas with the modern concept of advanced interstellar civilizations that may, in the opinion of some scientists, be keeping a benevolent watch over relatively primitive planets.

Thomas Chalmers' suggestions about angels were merely a hypothesis; he did not claim to believe it as fact, and he also dealt with other possibilities concerning the inhabitants of extrasolar planets. He was in no way antagonistic to science; in fact he said:

Who shall assign a limit to the discoveries of future ages? Who can prescribe to science her boundaries, or restrain the active and insatiable curiosity of man within the circle of present acquirements? We may guess with plausibility what we cannot anticipate with confidence. . . . To the men of other times we leave the full assurance of what we can assert with the highest probability, that yon planetary orbs are so many worlds, that they teem with life. . . .

Though this earth and these heavens were to disappear, there are other worlds that roll afar; the light of other suns shines upon them; and the sky which mantles them is garnished with other stars. Is it presumption to say that the moral world extends to these distant and unknown regions? that they are occupied with people? that the charities of home and neighbourhood flourish there?

These words are as relevant in our time as they were when Thomas Chalmers first spoke them in a crowded Scottish church over 150 years ago.

Both Thomas Paine's *Age of Reason* and Thomas Chalmers' *Astronomical Discourses* were directed to a wider audience than the works of philosophers, and both had extensive influence and appeal. Some people agreed with Paine. The great poet Shelley, who described innumerable solar systems in his poem "Queen Mab" and in his notes to it, was even more emphatic in his belief that existing religions were "irreconcilable with the knowledge of the stars." But on the whole, public opinion was on the side of Chalmers. Whichever side one favors, the two books, taken together, show well the awe and excitement shared by people of opposing views who reflected upon a vast, inhabited universe. Their great popularity in their time is easier to understand than the fact that they have been nearly forgotten; for similar emotions are shared by people of opposing views today.

chapter five

I was thinking this globe enough, till there sprang out
*   so noiseless around me myriads of other globes.*
Now, while the great thoughts of space and eternity fill
*   me, I will measure myself by them;*
And now, touch'd with the lives of other globes, arrived
*   as far along as those of the earth,*
Or waiting to arrive, or pass'd on farther than those of
*   the earth,*
I henceforth no more ignore them than I ignore my own
*   life,*
Or the lives of the earth arrived as far as mine, or wait-
*   ing to arrive.*

—Walt Whitman
Night on the Prairies (1860)

Perhaps the strangest controversy in the history of past opinion about extrasolar worlds began in 1853 when, for the first time, their reality was questioned not by a supporter of tradition, but by a man who admitted that his arguments were "not published without some fear of giving offence." He added, "It will be a curious . . . event, if it should now be deemed as blameable to doubt the existence of inhabitants of the Planets and Stars, as three centuries ago, it was held heretical to teach that doctrine."

It was no surprise to this author when his opinion aroused a furor. To a friend he had written, "I must publish my book without my name, in consequences of the heresies which it will thus contain." He did not mean heresies of the sort that had proved fatal to Bruno; it would not have been dangerous to sign his name to an unpopular view. But anonymous publication was

83

common in the nineteenth century, and he felt that because of his position it would be improper to become embroiled in something bound to stir up unfavorable publicity. He was already a noted figure. His name was William Whewell, and he was Master of Trinity College at England's Cambridge University. Furthermore, he had written distinguished books on the history and philosophy of science, and had in fact originated the term "scientist." Until William Whewell used that term, scientists had been called natural philosophers.

Because Dr. Whewell had written so much that was well known, his style was recognizable, and the fact that he was the author of the controversial book soon became an open secret. That did not matter; he had aimed not to hide his opinions, but simply to keep *Of the Plurality of Worlds: An Essay* separate from his more official works. The topic itself was considered neither sensational nor inappropriate for the head of a major college to discuss. What caused all the excitement was William Whewell's contention that there might be no intelligent beings on other planets, and that outside our solar system there might not even be any planets.

"We scarcely expected," said the London *Daily News,* "that in the middle of the nineteenth century, a serious attempt would have been made to restore the exploded ideas of man's supremacy over all other creatures in the universe; and still less that such an attempt would have been made by any one whose mind was stored with scientific truths. Nevertheless a champion has actually appeared, who boldly dares to combat against all the rational inhabitants of other spheres; and though as yet he wears his vizor down, his dominant bearing, and the peculiar dexterity and power with which he wields his arms, indicate that this knight-errant of nursery notions can be no other than the Master of Trinity College, Cambridge."

In a personal letter, Whewell said, "No one, so far as I know, has been the advocate of one world against many worlds, I mean in recent times." In the book, referring to the cosmological views presented in Thomas Chalmers' *Astronomical Discourses,* he wrote:

Such views are generally diffused in our time and country, are common to all classes of readers, and . . . are the *popular* views of persons of any degree of intellectual culture who have, directly or derivatively, accepted the doctrines of modern science. Among such persons, expressions which imply that the stars are globes of luminous matter, like the sun; that there are among them systems of revolving bodies, seats of life and intelligence; are so frequent and familiar that those who speak do not seem to be aware that, in using such expressions, they are making any assumption at all.

It was Dr. Whewell's avowed intent to show that people were indeed making assumptions, assumptions not warranted by the scientific evidence. Although he himself, in an earlier book called *Astronomy and General Physics,* had expressed the orthodox view, he had since come to the conclusion that science had no real proof for it. He was, of course, quite right. To the criticism, "Your arguments are merely negative. You only prove that we do not know the planets to be inhabited," he replied: "If, when I have proved that point, men were to cease to talk as if they knew that the planets *are* inhabited, I should have produced a great effect."

If he had left it at that, there might not have been so much angry debate. But William Whewell did not leave it there. He tried to prove that both science and religion supported the idea of Earth's uniqueness, and therefore both scientists and religious leaders found good grounds on which to oppose him. His biographer wrote, "Rarely in recent times has a book received so much attention from reviewers."

Nineteenth-century book reviews were long essays in themselves. Dr. Whewell's most vehement critic devoted forty pages of a well-known magazine to defending plurality of worlds, and still did not feel he had said enough; shortly afterwards he published a book of his own in rebuttal. Most of the other magazine reviews discussed the two books together. What was said in those reviews shows first, that belief in extrasolar planets

85

had indeed been considered unchallengeable; second, that the debate centered around issues that were largely irrelevant; and third, that almost everyone concerned was influenced more by emotion than logic.

The second book was by Sir David Brewster, an eminent Scottish physicist. Its title was *More Worlds than One: The Creed of the Philosopher and the Hope of the Christian.* As the subtitle suggest, Brewster—though a qualified scientist—based his arguments primarily on religious considerations. Actually, William Whewell did so too, but he was more subtle and more tolerant. He did not say that those who disagreed with him were motivated by "some morbid condition of the mental powers, which . . . delights in doing violence to sentiments deeply cherished, and to opinions universally believed," or by "a love of notoriety." Nor did he accuse them of "folly and irreverence towards the God of Nature." David Brewster used those phrases and similar ones. He asserted his opinions in an extremely dogmatic way. As one reviewer put it, "Sir David . . . is consequently continually laying himself open to attack. We regret to add that he is frequently deficient in common courtesy, and has allowed his temper and angry feelings to mingle in a discussion which is surely too remote from all meaner interests to deserve to be so sullied."

Both books made some valid points. Unfortunately, both also drew conclusions that did not follow from the arguments presented. In addition, both authors—despite their extensive knowledge of science—introduced dubious scientific hypotheses to back up predetermined opinions. They even made careless errors, which their antagonists were quick to point out. For example, Dr Whewell misstated the distance to the moon, illustrating it by saying that a month would be needed to get there at the ordinary speed of a railroad-carriage, whereas, according to one reviewer: "At thirty miles an hour, which is as fast as men wish to travel, it would take a little over three hundred and eighty-seven days."

Sir John Herschel, the son of Sir William Herschel and himself an astronomer of great fame, wrote after Dr. Whewell's death that the essay on plurality of worlds could "hardly be regarded as expressing his deliberate opinion.'' He felt that surely, as another astronomer put it, ''Whewell only advanced it in jest.'' This tells more about the opinion of Herschel and the scientists of his time than about William Whewell's opinion. Everything in the book and in his personal papers indicates that Whewell meant his ideas to be taken seriously. He maintained that many people were ''still troubled and dismayed at the doctrines of the vastness of the universe, and the multitude of worlds, which they suppose to be taught and proved by astronomy.'' His ''essay'' (which was nearly 300 pages long) suggests that he himself was one of those people.

Dr. Whewell used several main arguments, none of which could stand up under close scrutiny. He, and the reviewers, were most impressed by what he called the ''argument from geology.'' The discovery that the earth had evolved through many ages of past time, and that species of animals now extinct had existed in prehistoric eras, was a relatively new one. Whewell insisted that it countered the well-established belief that an uninhabited world would be wasted, for had not Earth itself been wasted for millions of years before man appeared? Some critics considered this idea ''very ingenious and striking,'' but most of them spotted the flaw in it. They pointed out that a world that was being *prepared* for intelligent life could not be called wasted since the ages of preparation on Earth had, presumably, been necessary. Sir David Brewster wrote:

> That is, *The Earth, the* ATOM OF SPACE, *is the only one of the planetary and sidereal worlds that is inhabited, because it was so long without inhabitants, and has occupied only an* ATOM OF TIME! If any of our readers see the force of this argument, they must possess an acuteness of perception to which we lay no claim. To us it is not only illogical;—it is a mere sound in the ear, without any sense in the brain. . . . Reason and common sense dictate a very different opinion. If *nearly infinity of time* has been employed to provide for intellectual and immortal life so glorious an abode, is it not probable that *nearly infinity* of space will be devoted to the same noble purpose?

This is a fair sample of Sir David's style; he was very fond of italics and capital letters. The same criticism was voiced more soberly by other men. And the issue was a significant one despite its irrelevance to the question of waste; for the first time, some people began to realize that planets might be at different stages of development.

The rest of the arguments Dr. Whewell employed were even less effective, although many reviewers got sidetracked and failed to note the deficiencies in them. What seems most peculiar today is that everybody on both sides assumed it was a matter of all or nothing. If *some* planets besides the earth were inhabited,or were becoming habitable, they *all* must be; if *some* stars were the centers of solar systems, then they *all* were—and vice versa. William Whewell contended that it was unlikely that double stars had planets, or that nebulae were composed of stars as most astronomers believed; to him, this seemed to point toward the conclusion that no other solar systems existed. David Brewster felt obliged to assert that double stars must have more complex systems of planets than single ones. The commentators took one position or the other. It did not occur to them that some stars besides our sun might have planets even if others had none.

The most hotly debated irrelevant question was the state of the planets in our own solar system. Dr. Whewell thought those planets uninhabitable; in this he was right, as far as is known today. But he was wrong in thinking that it had any bearing on the existence of habitable worlds in other solar systems. He certainly could not legitimately pronouce Earth unique on such grounds. Nevertheless, in his zeal to show that most planets were not abodes of life, he counted all 34 of the asteroids that were then known. His opponents, although in most cases willing to concede the asteroids and even the moons, were entirely unwilling to give up the primary planets. They agreed that their whole case would be weakened if even one ''useless'' world were to be acknowledged.

At the time of the Whewell/Brewster controversy, the evidence against habitation of the planets in our solar system was by no means conclusive. The following comment by an Oxford professor was justified:

The Essayist attempts to show that the ascertained conditions of the planetary bodies exclude the ascertained conditons of organic life . . . by the expressly-stated assumption that life is impossible except under conditions almost exactly similar to those under which we have an opportunity of studying it at the surface of our own planet. We think it a question whether this last position be a tenable one. Disguise it as we may, it comes in fact to this, that we may take our knowledge of what exists here for an exact measure of what may exist elsewhere. And in such an assumption there is considerable danger. It implies what we believe to be an exaggerated idea of the completeness of our physical knowledge.

Dr. Whewell held that to say animal life does not require the same environment on other planets as it does on ours would be to "run into the error which so long prevented many from accepting the Newtonian system:—the error of thinking that matter in the heavens is governed by quite different laws from matter on earth." This comparison was worth considering, and many present-day biologists might agree with it. But the professor argued that knowledge of the laws that govern organic life was "wholly and absolutely wanting," which in the 1850's was true. Moreover, Whewell could not say whether the environments of extrasolar worlds were like ours or not. He did not extend his principle of universal natural law into as wide a realm as those who believed in plurality of worlds; that was their chief weapon against him.

Perhaps the fairest estimate of Dr. Whewell's contribution was that of the reviewer who said, "Let us, then, conclude that the highly-gifted writer of this striking Essay has shown good grounds for a re-examination of the belief which has grown up by such gradual and imperceptible steps into a religion amongst us, that there are MEN in other worlds."

*

However, no widespread reexamination of the belief in other worlds occurred as the result of Whewell's book. Most people did not want to stop believing. "There is no subject within the whole range of knowledge so universally interesting as that of a Plurality of Worlds," wrote Sir David Brewster in the introduction to *More Worlds Than One.* "It commands the sympathies, and appeals to the judgment of men of all nations, of all creeds, and of all times."

Although as usual, Sir David may have somewhat overstated the case, this declaration was—and still is—substantially true. During eras not dominated by contrary ideas, people have tended toward a conviction that mankind is not alone. Some well-known nineteenth century figures recorded their opinions on the subject. Alfred Tennyson, whose poetry contains many references to other solar systems besides those on pages 2 and 152, wrote of Whewell's *Essay:* "It is to me anything but a satisfactory book. It is inconceivable that the whole Universe was merely created for us who live in this third-rate planet of a third-rate sun."

William Whewell had been Tennyson's tutor at Cambridge University. That was long before Dr. Whewell began to doubt the existence of other inhabited worlds, and there is no way of knowing whether the two ever discussed the subject. But young Alfred was interested in it even then, for the poem *Timbuctoo* (from which the title of this book, *The Planet-Girded Suns,* is taken) was written while he was in college and it won the Cambridge Prize Medal. He had competed for the prize only to please his father; he did not really think the poem good enough, and later, when he became poet laureate of England, he did not include it in collected volumes of his work.

About the same time Alfred Tennyson was attending college in England, Ralph Waldo Emerson—later renowned as a philosopher and poet—was gaining fame as a young minister in America. Among the few of his sermons that have been published is one that dealt with "all the worlds of God":

To suppose that the constitution of the race of yesterday that now plants the fields of this particular planet, should be the pattern for all the orders that people the huge globes in the heaven is too improbable to be entertained. Rather believe that the benignant Power which has assigned each creature to its own element, the fish to the sea, the bird to the air, the beast to the field, has not less nicely adjusted elsewhere his creatures to their habitation. . . .

We are assured in any speculation we may indulge concerning the tenants of other regions . . . the moral law, justice and mercy would be at home in every climate and world where life is; that we can go nowhere but wisdom will not be valuable . . . truth, sacred, and charity divine. . . . We then feel that there is no grandeur like moral grandeur. Before one act of courage, of love, of self devotion, all height and distance are ineffectual and the stars withdraw their shining. This only is real, absolute, independent of all circumstance and all change.

Another man who had a good deal to say about life on extrasolar worlds was the Danish scientist Hans Christian Oersted, the discoverer of electromagnetism. At a meeting of Scandinavian philosophers in 1844 he said, "He who is convinced by the proofs I have mentioned, that living beings are distributed through the whole of existence, will contemplate the stars with very different thoughts and views, and have a far wider field for the scope of his imagination than he who is ignorant of these secrets of nature."

Oersted believed that "futurity promises to reveal still more secrets" and that "we are not isolated beings, but . . . are related to the whole universe." The next year, at a meeting of scientists, he gave a long speech arguing that the principles of intelligence, beauty and morality were the same on all worlds. He concluded it with his hope that this world would be continually gaining more knowledge, which would give "a much deeper insight of what happens on distant planets," and suggested that the same would happen there with regard to ours.

The idea of unity among all the intelligent inhabitants of the cosmos was fairly widespread in the first half of the nineteenth century. Today this seems a very modern concept, one that people are only now beginning to take seriously. Yet even in the 1830's and 1840's some gave deep thought to it. Among them was a clergyman named Thomas Dick, who wrote several popular books about plurality of worlds including one called "Celestial Scenery." In speculating on differences in species based on their environments he concluded that if a planet's atmosphere was invisible, it was "purer" than ours and that the "moral and physical condition" of such planets' inhabitants was therefore "probably superior to what is enjoyed upon earth." At the same time, however, he maintained, "Truth, and every branch of knowledge by which the mind of a rational being can be adorned, must be *substantially* the same in every world throughout the amplitudes of creation."

On the next page he went still further, with comments astonishingly farsighted:

Whether we may ever enjoy an intimate correspondence with beings belonging to other worlds, is a question which will frequently obtrude itself on a contemplative mind. It is evident that, in our present state, all direct intercourse with other worlds is impossible. The law of gravitation, which unites all the worlds in the universe in one grand system, separates man from his kindred spirits in other planets, and interposes an impassable barrier to his excursions to distant regions, and to his correspondence with other orders of intellectual beings. But in the present state he is only in the *infancy of his being.* . . .

He will, doubtless, be brought into contact and correspondence with numerous orders of kindred beings, with whom he may be permitted to associate on terms of equality and of endearing friendship. All the virtuous intelligences throughout creation may be considered as members of one *great family* . . . and it is not improbable that it is one grand design of the Deity to promote a regular and progressive intercourse among the several branches of his intelligent offspring, though at distant intervals and in divers manners, and after the lapse of long periods of duration.

Such an intercouse may be necessary . . . to the full expansion of the moral and intellectual faculties, and to the acquisition of all that knowledge which relates to . . . the physical and moral government of the universe. For this purpose it may be necessary that branches of the universal family that have existed in different periods of duration, and in regions widely separated from each other, should be brought into mutual association, that they may communicate to each other the results of their knowledge and experience.

The ideas Dr. Dick expressed there bear a striking resemblance to recent speculations about galactic federations of worlds. Not even science fiction had then ventured to suggest the underlying thought that must have prompted his statements: the thought of a universal family of mortal peoples, destined to eventually communicate through some inconceivable means, and to share knowledge gained through varied experience "on terms of equality."

Today, scientists who are devising mathematical codes suitable for interstellar communication would find nothing outdated in that passage from the voluminous writings of Dr. Dick. Some such scientists would not agree with the part about Deity, while others would—but in either case the rest would seem highly relevant.

There is no indication that anyone besides Thomas Dick thought actual contact between solar systems might ever be feasible, let alone that it might be a necessary feature of cosmic design. His readers, if they interpreted what he said in that light, do not appear to have adopted the thought; and it did not arise again until much, much later. The feeling of universal kinship, considered apart from hope of contact, was more common.

In the American poet Walt Whitman it was particularly strong. He wrote, "It is not enough to have this globe, or a certain time—I will have thousands of globes, and all time." Many of his poems express this feeling. For example, in *Kosmos* he said:

93

Who, out of the theory of the earth, and of his or her body,
understands by subtle analogies all other theories. . . .

Who believes not only in our globe, with its sun and moon, but
in other globes, with their suns and moons;

Who, constructing the house of himself or herself, not for a
day, but for all the time, sees races, eras, dates, generations,

The past, the future, dwelling there, like space, inseparable
together.

Walt Whitman was one of the first prominent men to think of
worlds and their intelligent species as being at various stages of
evolution. Although evolutionary concepts of planetary formation, of geology, and to a lesser extent of biology, had been
discussed by a number of thinkers for some years, the vast
majority of people still pictured everything in the universe as
having been created simultaneously. If they accepted the evidence of fossils as proof of a long period of development on
Earth, they tended to assume that development on alien
planets—both in our solar system and in others—had reached
exactly the same stage. There was no general change in public
opinion about this until the 1870's.

*

The issue of-evolution, which brought new ways of thinking,
was complex. It was not merely a matter of whether man did or
did not descend from the apes. Long before controversy arose
over the origin of man, there was debate over evolutionary
theories of cosmogony and geology. Early supporters of those
theories did not suggest that similar ideas of gradual change
applied to the physical characteristics of intelligent beings. They
viewed man (and the inhabitants of other worlds also) as essen-
tially different from animal species, even when the basic principle of evolution was extended to organic life. They agreed with
opponents of this principle that a planet was designed and
prepared for the benefit of its inhabitants, however long the

process might take; and usually they assumed the planet's environment to have been made to fit the inhabitants' needs rather than the reverse. In other words, to them the question was not why man was comfortable with the amount of heat and light received from the sun, but why Earth was at the proper distance from the sun for his comfort.

During the latter part of the nineteenth century this outlook was challenged. Scientists began to investigate the possibility that Earth's environment might have had an effect on man's development. One result of the new attitude was acceptance of the idea that Earth's position in the universe was no more central in terms of time than in terms of space.

"It appears to me," wrote the astronomer Richard Anthony Proctor, "that the belief that life in this earth corresponds with a period special for the universe itself is as monstrous as the old belief that our earth is the centre of the universe."

Richard Proctor was especially interested in other worlds, and in the 1870's he wrote many books and articles about them. He also lectured to hundreds of audiences in both Great Britain and America. Commenting on this experience, he said, "None save astronomers, and few only of those, care for researches into the star-depths, except in connnection with the thought that every star is a sun, and therefore probably the light and fire of a system of worlds like those which circle around our own sun."

In an article and in his book *Our Place Among Infinities,* Proctor presented what he called "a new theory of life in other worlds," which he contrasted to the opposing "Whewellite" and "Brewsterian" theories. "Men have not been so bold in widening their conceptions of time as in widening their conceptions of space," he wrote. "It is here and thus that, in my judgment, the subject of life in other worlds has been hitherto incorrectly dealt with." He went on to say:

Brewster and Dick and Chalmers, all in fact who have taken that doctrine under their special protection, reason respecting other worlds as though, if they failed to prove that other orbs are inhabited *now,* or are at least *now* supporting life in some way or other, they failed of their purpose altogether. The idea does not seem to have occurred to them that there is room . . . in eternity of time not only for activity but for rest.

The Whewellite theory, Proctor continued, was "not held in very great favour." He felt that even those who, like himself, did not think "the ways and works of God are to be judged by our conceptions of the fitness of things" preferred the Brewsterian theory. "Nevertheless," he said, "we must be guided in these matters by evidence, not by sentiment—by facts, not by our feelings. It is well, therefore, to note that the decision does not lie between the two theories which have just been dealt with."

More than twenty years had passed since the publication of Whewell's book and Brewster's reply to it. From the modern viewpoint, the delay in recognition of the third alternative is difficult to understand. It seems strange that Richard Proctor considered it a "new theory," for he had studied the subject thoroughly and must have been aware that the possibility of not all planets being ready for habitation had been mentioned; in fact he had mentioned it himself in earlier works. But apparently not even he had seen the implications before. His ideas do not seem to have been thought revolutionary or startling, and his name is not prominent in the history of science. His theory may merely have spelled out what others were beginning to grasp:

This present time . . . is a random selection, so to speak, regarded with reference to the existence of life in any other world, and being a random selection, it is much more likely to belong to the period when there is no life there. . . . This applies to the planets of our solar system only in so far as we are ignorant of their conditions. . . . As respects the members of those systems of worlds which circle, as we believe (from analogy) around other suns than ours, the probability that any particular world is inhabited at this present time is exceedingly small. . . . Have we then been led to the Whewellite theory that our earth is the sole abode of life? Far from it. . . . The very argument from probability which leads us to regard any given sun as not the centre of a scheme in which at this moment there is life, forces upon us the conclusion that among . . . the millions of suns which people pace, millions have orbs circling around them which are at this present time the abode of living creatures.

This seems obvious because it is so close to current theories; it seems to belong to the 1970's instead of the 1870's. Yet Proctor was by no means a hundred years ahead of his time. On the contrary, he was quite representative of it. Between his outlook and today's came a long era of upheaval, a time of changing views and disturbing thoughts in many fields of knowledge. Few positive statements can be made about the effects of these changes on the idea of plurality of worlds. But it is a fact—and in many ways a strange one—that what had not happened in Whewell's era did happen later. Gradually, as the nineteenth century ended and the twentieth began, people abandoned the conviction that habitable planets circle the stars. A still stranger fact is that they forgot such a conviction had ever been prevalent.

Some of the reasons for the shifts in opinion during the century just past are known. For example, it is definitely known why astronomers revised their estimates of how many stars are likely to have planets, and why they later returned to estimates closer to those of the nineteenth century. Yet these reasons do not appear to fully account for the reversal of people's attitudes toward the existence of *some* inhabited worlds. They surely do not account for previous opinions having been forgotten.

Most scientists today who are interested in extrasolar life would be surprised by what the eighteenth and nineteenth-century scholars wrote about it. Even they do not realize how widespread a concept it used to be. One of them, a Fellow of the Royal Astronomical Society, recently wrote, "Starting at the turn of the century with H.G.Wells' famous *War of the Worlds,* we have been nurtured in the belief that the wandering planets . . . might contain beings of an intelligent kind." But though H.G.Wells' science fiction was certainly very popular, more *nonfiction* expressed this belief before Wells wrote it than afterwards. The same present-day astronomer maintained, "It is only within comparatively recent times that the general idea of planets existing at interstellar distances has come to be accepted." Similar statements are to be found in many recent science books.

This is not to say that today's astronomers ought to know better, for unless they have time to seek out books and magazines of the past—which busy scientists do not—they are not likely to come across any information on the subject. Nor should historians be criticized. Historians write only about things they consider important, and extrasolar worlds were not considered important at the time most modern historians received their education in science.

The significance of statements like the one above is that they prove that somewhere between the 1870's and the 1970's, there is a puzzling gap in the story of man's view of other solar systems.

chapter six

What links are ours with orbs that are
So resolutely far.   . . .
*   Implacable they shine*
To us who would of Life obtain
An answer for the life we strain
*   To nourish with one sign.*
Nor can imagination throw
The penetrative shaft: we pass
The breath of thought, who would divine
*   If haply they may grow*
As Earth; have our desire to know;
If life comes there to grain from grass,
And flowers like ours of toil and pain.

—George Meredith
Meditation Under Stars (1888)

Many factors may have contributed to the decline of belief in
extrasolar worlds, but not all can be positively identified. The
scientific issues are easiest to define. In the first place, the 1870's
marked a shift in scientific interests. Something happened that
made astronomers—and also laymen who were enthusiastic
about astronomy—forget other solar systems to concentrate on
ours. The planet Mars was in an unusually favorable position for
observation in 1877, and in that year the famous "canals" were
seen. The man who observed them, an Italian, used the word
canali, which means simply "grooves" or "channels," but
English-speaking people quickly adopted the word "canals"
with its unmistakable implication of an engineering feat of
intelligent beings. Naturally, the supposition of a nearby, visible
extraterrestrial civilization far outshone conjectures about distant,
invisible ones. The controversy continued for many years. Not

all observers could see the markings, and not all scientists thought that they were artificial even when they did see them. Still, the attention of those concerned about plurality of worlds was thoroughly occupied.

Another reason astronomers began to lose interest in extrasolar worlds was their increasing knowledge of conditions on our own solar system's planets. This knowledge, combined with growing knowledge of biology, tended to discourage the idea that all planets were habitable—although many still maintained that forms of life unlike Earth's might exist in alien environments. Moreover, it led to a feeling that declarations not based on solid evidence were unjustified.

That, of course, was exactly what William Whewell had insisted long before. Before, however, there had been little more evidence about the observable planets than about invisible ones. This was no longer true. Furthermore, in the late nineteenth century science of all types had become so excited by its recent discoveries that it held there could be few discoveries left to make. The prevalent opinion was that all that could ever be known was already known, and that nothing remained but to fill in details. In medieval times there had been a similar reaction to Aristotelian science; just as had happened then, people turned away from the thought of a realm beyond the knowable.

In 1882 the American astronomer Simon Newcomb, in a book called *Popular Astronomy,* wrote:

> Many thinking people regard the discovery of evidences of life in other worlds as the great ultimate object of telescopic research. It is, therefore, extremely disappointing to learn that the attainment of any direct evidence of such life seems entirely hopeless—so hopeless, indeed, that it has almost ceased to occupy the attention of astronomers. The spirit of modern science is wholly adverse to speculation on questions for the solution of which no scientific evidence is attainable.

In Newcomb's case, this simply introduced speculation of his own. He himself was willing to state in conclusion, "The probabilities· are in favor of only a very small fraction of the planets being peopled with intelligent beings. But when we reflect that the possible number of the planets is counted by hundreds of millions, this small fraction may be really a very large number, and among this number many may be peopled by beings much higher than ourselves in the intellectual scale." That, like some of Richard Proctor's statements, could as well have been said today as nearly a hundred years ago. However, reluctance of professional astronomers to give opinions was common during most of the interval.

One major cause of this was that astronomers, like other scientists, stopped explaining their theories in religious terms. Always before, when they lacked observational data, scientists had not hesitated to discuss religion. There had been no distinction between "science" and "natural philosophy"; the word "scientist" had not even existed until William Whewell invented it in 1840. But near the end of the nineteenth century science became fully established as a limited field kept separate from other forms of theorizing.

Experimental and observational science had no need to rely on religious arguments; but the part of "natural philosophy" concerned with plurality of worlds coud not employ experimental methods. Observation yielded certain results—especially after the invention of the spectroscope proved that the stars were composed of the same elements as the sun—but it could not give an answer to the question of whether extraterrestrial life did or did not exist. That question had always lain in the province of religion for the very reason that it was unanswerable.

Though like all religious questions, the issue of other worlds had involved controversy, there had been one thing everyone agreed about: the principle of purpose. Nobody had thought of questioning whether such worlds had a purpose; only a few had ventured to suggest that their purpose might be impossible to determine. By and large, it had been believed that the obvious purpose of a planet was to provide a home for inhabitants. But in the late nineteenth century this argument for habitation was abandoned. Scientists abandoned it because of the newly drawn line between science and religion. People in general abandoned it because they were beginning to doubt the whole idea of a purposeful universe.

Back in 1855, the Oxford professor who reviewed William Whewell's book on the plurality of worlds had made a prophetic remark. He had said, "If the planets are not made for inhabitants . . . since some of them are of no use to us, and are not likely to be of any, it appears that there are things created without any use at all. And this is a dangerous element to admit upon so large a scale into our calculation of the evidence for design."

Like earlier writers, Whewell's opponents had argued with great vehemence in their effort to avoid this danger. It had not been considered an exclusively religious matter then. As one American magazine put it, "Common-sense, popular instinct, so believes to-day, from its undoubting creed, that *all things exist for* USE." Whewell himself had never denied that; he had merely maintained that not all purposes were known. To the science of his time, which was based on the assumption that the universe was well-designed, the thought of things "without any use at all" did indeed seem dangerous.

This danger was a real one, though like all dangers accompanying the advance of human knowledge, it was unavoidable. The progress of science revealed many things that existed without apparent purpose. For instance, theories of organic evolution revealed that some forms of life exist briefly but lack the ability to survive. These theories were also linked with ideas of randomness and of probability expressed in statistical terms. Such concepts were foreign to the mid-century mind, and disturbing to many people who found them in later decades' discussions about the likelihood of intelligent life on extrasolar planets. It became more and more evident that the moon was not habitable, and there was no assurance that supposedly younger planets in our own system ever would be. Mars offered hope, yet even if Mars were inhabited, some "wasted worlds" would remain.

Richard Proctor, one of the last professional astronomers to consider the question of purpose relevant, wrote:

Recognizing in our own world, in many instances, what to our ideas resembles waste—waste seeds, waste lives . . . waste regions, waste forces—recognizing superfluity and superabundance in all the processes and in all the works of nature, should it not appear at least possible that some, perhaps even a large proportion, of the worlds in the multitudinous systems peopling space, are not only not now supporting life, but never have supported life and never will? . . . May not we without irreverence conceive (as higher beings than ourselves may *know*) that a planet or a sun may fail in the making?

It is not possible to say just what role people's attitudes toward plurality of worlds played in twentieth-century society's skepticism toward pattern and purpose in the universe. The change was partly a result of such skepticism—but also, perhaps, a partial clause. When people have been told for two hundred years that a cosmos full of perfectly ordered solar systems is evidence of the wisdom of its design, they do not like to hear about planets and suns having failed in the making.

Proctor, unlike many, went on to say that even in the case of "failures" there might be uses he and his contemporaries were unable to conceive. And that, of course, was true. The issue is not a dead one. Proof that it is not can be seen in the following words of Sir David Brewster, who in trying to refute one of William Whewell's arguments made a point he could never have imagined. Whewell compared planets to islands, saying that if people who lived on one island had never traveled to any others, they could not reasonably assume that the others were inhabited, or that it was an indication of poor design for them to be left uninhabited. Sir David replied:

We know of hundreds of islands without inhabitants. We can assign also a very good reason why they were made, and why they are not inhabited, and if we were to be assured of the fact, it would excite no surprise whatever. We could not say that God therefore made them in vain, because when the art of navigation is discovered, they may be found to contain gold and silver, coal and iron, and excellent harbours.

Now that the art of space navigation has been discovered—and a means of interstellar travel, though not discovered, is at least within man's conception—the idea of "wasted" worlds is no longer a valid argument against universal purpose. Many people today, whether they believe in a Creator or not, believe that uninhabited planets will provide rich resources and, eventually, "excellent harbours" for emigrants from this overcrowded island world.

*

Just after the turn of the century, in 1903, another book appeared that challenged the idea of other inhabited worlds. It presented too extreme a view to gain wide acceptance, but it impressed people because of the reputation of its author. He was Alfred Russel Wallace, a famous naturalist who had developed theories related to Darwin's. When he wrote *Man's Place in the Universe* he was eighty years old. The magazine *Scientific American* said, "When Dr. Wallace asserts that our earth is the sole abode of life in the universe . . . one school claims that he is old and in his dotage; the other, that he has become wise in his old age."

Dr. Wallace's opinion was much the same as Dr. Whewell's had been fifty years before, although his arguments were different because of the progress of science during these years, and also because he did not base them on religion. "The old idea that all the planets were inhabited, and that all the stars existed for the sake of other planets, which planets existed to develop life, would, in the light of our present knowledge, seem utterly improbable and incredible," he wrote. He maintained that Earth was probably "the only inhabited planet, not only in the Solar System but in the whole stellar universe."

Though Alfred Wallace claimed that this was the logical result of the latest astronomical theories, most astronomers did not agree with him. His views were "received with general surprise and considerable disfavor,'' for he attempted to prove that Earth really was in the physical center of the universe after all—that is, that Earth's solar system was. He held that only in the approximate center could conditions be right for intelligent life to evolve, a theory for which he had no evidence. There was no wide concurrence that our sun was as close to the middle of the universe as he thought, or that it would stay there long even if it were.

As usual, however, readers got sidetracked by the matter of life on the other planets within our solar system, an issue that Dr. Wallace, as an authority on organic evolution, was better qualified to discuss. He pointed out reasons why they were not only uninhabited at present, but could never become inhabited. Although by no means everyone accepted his conclusion, the trend of scientific progress was in its favor. And on the whole, people who were attracted by the thought of beings on other worlds wanted to envision them on the nearby ones; evidence against that was discouraging to them. This may have led some to go along with Wallace when he said:

> It may, and I believe will, turn out, that of all the myriad stars, the more we learn about them, the smaller and smaller will become the scanty residue which, with any probability, we can suppose to illuminate and vivify habitable earths. And when with this scanty probability we combine the still scantier probability that any such planet will possess simultaneously, and for a sufficiently long period, *all* the highly complex and delicately balanced conditions known to be essential for a full life-development, the conception that on this earth alone has such development been completed will not seem so wildly improbable a conjecture as it has hitherto been held to be.

There was resistance to such pronouncements even among those who accepted them. "We must make the best of it, even if we are doomed to undergo the worst of it," wrote one reviewer. "It must be said, however, that this book . . . is not a cheerful message, and we could wish it had been briefer. As one reads along its clear pages, and between the lines finds not only the doom of mankind, but the universe vacant of life . . . one asks why the proof is piled so high. . . . . So intolerable is the despair that settles upon us that we instinctively protest against Mr. Wallace's limitation within the Milky Way, and assert that every system, in its evolutionary process, must produce a planet that repeats every physical and human phase of our own. A planet may die, but a lifeless universe!—'that way madness lies.' ''

The idea that suns change, and planets do become unable to support life, had been discussed for some time; during the early twentieth century it became a basic part of people's thinking about astronomy. The prospect of doom for our solar system was, of course, a distant one—millions of years in the future —that nobody actually worried about. Yet combined with the increasing reluctance of scientists to affirm the existence of better and happier civilizations in other systems, its implications were definitely not cheerful.

Most astronomers continued to state that extrasolar worlds probably existed, though they felt, more and more, that not all stars were accompanied by them. A 1903 article in *Popular Astronomy* declared:

> It is unreasonable and illogical to say that matter operated upon by a universal law will produce results that are substantially different. . . . Assuming for the average of all other suns visible in the universe but one dark body each, and the result will be to people space with a hundred million other planets. It is equally unreasonable and illogical to say that not one of that mighty array, in the process of its physical development, has produced a single instance of germ life. Let us rather nourish the belief, the hope, that there are other eyes than ours to view the splendors of this universe, other intellects to grapple with its profound problems, other hearts to pulsate and joy under the kindly influences of love.

That was still the orthodox opinion at the beginning of the twentieth century. In a lecture for children given at Christmas of 1913, a professor of astronomy from Oxford University said,

"All the thousands of millions of stars in the sky may be suns like ours, and each of them may have many planets circling round it as we circle the sun, and yet Mr. Alfred Russel Wallace sincerely believes that there is not a sign of life on one of them!'' The professor was talking to the children about life on Mars; he said there was evidence on both sides of the question and he had not made up his mind about it. "At least I have not made it up about Mars," he continued. "On the big question raised by Mr. Wallace, whether our little Earth is the only place for life, I have made it up; I don't think for a moment that it is. I have read his book carefully, but cannot see that he makes out a case for so strange an idea. That there is plenty of life elsewhere seems to me practically certain."

*

But major changes were beginning to shake the realm of science. Its neat, orderly mechanical cosmos had been upset in the late nineteenth century by the concept of evolution. More recently, concepts of a still more startling kind had been introduced. Newton's laws had been found not to embody the last word on the structure of the universe; the theory of relativity had revolutionized the field of physics. Soon to come was something called the Uncertainty Principle, which, though connected with atoms rather than cosmology, had the effect its name suggest.

Science no longer assumed that there was nothing knowable left to determine. Nor was it at all sure what was knowable. Only things that could be verified seemed worth studying. Astronomers built more powerful telescopes and found new techniques of observation, through which they were able to gain a great deal of information about stars and galaxies. They could gain no more information about planets. So speculation about planets was, for the most part, abandoned.

One question concerning planets did receive attention, however, and that was the problem of their origin. From the late eighteenth century until the beginning of the twentieth, the nebular hypothesis of planetary formation had been generally accepted by science. According to that theory, solar systems were formed when gaseous nebulae condensed. But there were mathematical difficulties with the nebular hypothesis. In the early twentieth century increased knowledge made it impossible to ignore those difficulties, and a new theory was developed. The new theory declared that planets were formed only when two stars passed very close to each other, so close that matter was pulled out of one sun by gravitational tides. It was calculated that such an event could occur in our galaxy no more frequently than about once in five thousand million years.

This calculation, which "proved" planetary systems to be extremely rare, was based upon the laws of chance. Planets had previously been thought to come into being as a normal step in the development of stars. That idea was given up; it seemed self-evident that they were the result of unlikely accidents. Stars were obviously too far apart to have near-collisions very often. At least once, someone suggested that the meeting of two stars might not be a chance occurrence, but there was no evidence for thinking it was anything else. The only grounds for such a belief were those associated with purpose, and discussion of purpose had become—as one writer put it—"largely taboo in science to-day."

Though such discussion was no longer within the scope of science, no more revealing methods had yet replaced it. And "chance" was a convenient explanation for anything that could not be explained by scientists' current theories. Biologists as well as astronomers asserted that the chance of intelligent life having evolved elsewhere was so slight as to be almost negligible. They did not know the origin of life. Some tried to explain it by saying that living spores were carried from one planet to another by meteorites, or that such spores simply came out of space; but the assumptions this theory demanded were debatable. Moreover, it merely put the problem back a stage, for how had the living spores originally come to be? Many concluded that the evolution of life on a world was wholly accidental. Sometimes the word "freak" was used.

The theory that planets were produced by the near approach of two stars was the accepted one in astronomy from the first decade of this century until about the time the Second World War ended.

The statistical probability of there being planets circling any given star was therefore judged to be slight. That alone, however, was not enough to account for the decline of belief in existence of other solar systems. All the astronomers who wrote about the subject admitted that in view of the millions of stars in our galaxy, and the countless other galaxies in the cosmos, statistics made plain that there must be a great many planetary systems despite the supposed infrequency of their formation. In 1939 the magazine *Scientific Monthly* said:

> The question, you will note, centers upon the probable number of planetary systems per million or billion of suns rather than upon the likelihood that our particular system has no near-counterpart in space. Most astronomers to-day are inclined to think that a planetary family is a comparatively rare phenonenon in space; but probably no one would make the statement stronger than that. Certainly the whole burden of proof would rest upon the rash theorist who would make our solar system unique in the universe.

Yet several well-known astronomers had already made their statements about the rarity of planets stronger—at least, they had given the idea a stronger impact in their writings. For this among other reasons, the majority of people discounted the *number* of solar systems still thought probable; they were overwhelmed by the huge *proportion* of stars considered planetless. Such a reaction seems to have been shared by scientists themselves.

A factor in this may have been that they felt disillusioned, and perhaps a bit sheepish, on account of the failure to discover any intelligent life on Mars. From the time of the first observation of the so-called "canals" until the close approach of Mars in 1924, some had great hopes of really finding evidence of Martians. When no evidence appeared, they turned away from the thought of extraterrestrial life altogether, though there were no real grounds for doing so on that basis. "The little planet Mars is seen to have been given undue significance," the *Scientific Monthly* article went on. "It seems to have life, but if this is a mistake, it doesn't much matter after all. . . . If Mars is as dead as the proverbial doornail, we can still look outward with confidence that blind chemical forces have not cast us up as living accidents on the huge dead banks of eternity. Somewhere in space are many, many fellow-travelers on the brief but hopeful trek of life.''

Nevertheless, hope was not a fashionable outlook at that time. The nineteenth century had been a predominantly optimistic period, but during the first half of the twentieth, there were disillusionments far worse than those connected with Mars. The First World War and the Depression did not leave people in a hopeful frame of mind. It was common for the universe to be thought unfriendly, and the views emphasized by the most popular scientific writers were grim.

In the seventeenth century, also a time of upheaval, people had believed that the earth was slowly but surely decaying. In the early twentieth century a great deal was said about ''heat death,'' or the ultimate ''running down'' of the universe as a result of the Second Law of Thermodynamics. ''A running-down universe—a universe inevitably and irrevocably deteriorating . . . and we men as utterly insignificant in comparison with its immensities and hopelessly impotent to stay the impending doom—it is of such a universe that we form a picture in our minds as we read the latest pronouncements of astronomy,'' declared one magazine.

This, like the seventeenth-century belief in decay, may have something in common with today's fears about Earth being permanently ruined by pollution. Science cannot predict the future; it can only form theories based on the facts at hand. During eras of change and discouraging problems, pessimistic theories have generally spread more widely than optimistic ones.

Among the originators of the theory that planets form only after a close encounter between two stars was the eminent astronomer Sir James Jeans. He had a high reputation as a scientist, but he was best known to the general public as the author of best-selling books for laymen. The science in his books was accurate, although it is now outdated. But the impression people got from them was less accurate. Sir James presented personal feelings along with information, and readers did not always distinguish between these feelings and proven scientific facts.

"Above all else, we find the universe terrifying because it appears to be indifferent to life like our own," James Jeans wrote. "Perhaps indeed we ought to say it appears to be actively hostile to life. . . . Into such a universe we have stumbled, if not exactly by mistake, at least as the result of what may properly be described as an accident." Since on the pages immediately following, he went on to discuss the rarity of planets in scientific terms, many people naturally assumed that the first statement represented the official opinion of scientists.

The books and articles of James Jeans were full of phrases like, "We, the only thinking beings, so far as we know, in the whole of space," and "At the best, life must be limited to a tiny fraction of the universe." Nor was he the only notable astronomer to make such statements. Sir Arthur Eddington, another distinguished scientist who wrote for the general public, said in a 1928 issue of *Harper's Magazine:*

> If the planets of the solar system should fail us, there remain some thousands of millions of stars which we have been accustomed to regard as suns ruling attendant systems of planets. It has seemed a presumption, bordering almost on impiety, to deny them life of the same order of creation as ourselves. It would indeed be rash to assume that nowhere else has Nature repeated the strange experiment which she has performed on the earth. But there are considerations which must hold us back from populating the universe too liberally. . . .
>
> The solar system is not the typical product of development of a star; it is not even a common variety of development; it is a freak. . . . I do not think that the whole purpose of the Creation has been staked on the one planet where we live; and in the long run we cannot deem ourselves the only race that has been or will be gifted with the mystery of consciousness. But I feel inclined to claim that *at the present time* our race is supreme; and not one of

the profusion of stars in their myriad clusters looks down on scenes comparable to those which are passing beneath the rays of the sun.

He "felt inclined to claim" earth's supremacy; he made no claim that scientific evidence demanded such a view. Yet from the 1920's until quite recently, that was the view that predominated.

*

Nevertheless, proof that many qualified astronomers continued to assume sentient life must exist beyond our solar system can be found in scientific journals of the 1920's and 1930's, as well as in the earlier ones. In 1921, for example, a debate was carried on in *Science,* the journal of the American Association for the Advancement of Science. There were letters to the editor on both sides of the question, but even the most vehement opponents of extrasolar life maintained only that no evidence for it had been obtained. They did not say that the existence of *any* inhabited planets besides Earth was improbable.

The general public, however, did not read scientific journals. It may be that there were people who did not like to express their opinions for fear of being thought "unscientific." They may have heard the statements of men like Sir James Jeans second or third hand, and missed the statistics that showed our solar system was considered a rare phenomenon rather than a unique one.

Certainly there was public interest in plurality of worlds during the period when the idea lacked general scientific support. That may have been part of the problem. Among the most ardent defenders of extrasolar life, once scientists stopped committing themselves to unprovable details, were people interested in spiritualism and extrasensory perception: areas that in the early twentieth century had no scientific approval at all. In the popular mind, "guilt by association" may have reduced plurality of worlds to the same category. It came to be viewed as a subject fascinating for fiction, but not quite respectable if taken seriously—as some tend to view it even now.

Therefore, far fewer respected writers published nonfiction

about other solar systems than had done so in previous eras. One was the French author Camille Flammarion, who wrote many such books in the last decades of the nineteenth century but also some in the twentieth. He was an extreme enthusiast who believed passionately in innumerable worlds and described their environments in somewhat more detail than was wise from the scientific standpoint, especially the many-colored suns—but the public loved his work. It was widely read and some was translated into English.

Another European speculator about extrasolar worlds was Maurice Maeterlinck, who is best known to young people as the author of the fairy tale *The Children's Blue Bird*. Maeterlinck discussed superior civilizations in several essays. He felt that beings far in advance of man must surely possess the ability to become disembodied spirits in order to travel from world to world, and he was convinced that any such being who came to Earth and observed the suffering of its people would do something about it. "Having for centuries surpassed what our medical science has not even begun to discover, he knows all the sovereign remedies," Maeterlinck declared, "and he has only to say a word in order to abolish all these torments. . . . If we were in his place, should we hesitate a moment?" Then, pointing out that no intervention from another world ever had abolished suffering on this planet, he asked despairingly, "Is there not reason to fear that we are for ever alone in the universe, and that no other world has ever been more intelligent or better than our own?"

These are legitimate questions, and timely ones. They are being asked today by those who envision travel by means of starships as well as by believers in disembodied spirits, and are also being raised in scientific discussions of interstellar communication. There are many possible answers. Maeterlinck himself, in a later essay, said that maybe ancient intervention had indeed occurred, or that spiritual radiations, similar to the physical ones science had discovered, might pass between planets through space. In regard to why suffering on Earth had not been abolished, he concluded:

113

And even if one of these stars had attained the goal for which we strive, had at last learned all: the laws, the origin, the aim of the universe, the idea that underlies it; what could such a star do, what could we do, were we in its place? Can knowledge of what the laws are bring with it the power to change them? . . . Would victory over time and space give mastery over what inspired them, give the power to modify, the power to change? Perhaps; but then we should be like unto the God whom we glimpse through the semblence of things; and what He has been unable or unwilling to do, we should not do either.

Others besides Maeterlinck proposed theories of ''spiritual radiation,'' which was conceived as something like ESP. Prior to the Second World War the idea of *physical* contacts among solar systems was confined almost exclusively to fiction. Near the end of the nineteenth century there was talk about communication by signals with Martians, but interstellar communication did not enter anyone's mind. Though travel by spaceship within our solar system began to receive serious attention in the 1920's, only a minority considered it more than a dream inspired by science fiction voyages to the moon and Mars; and physical journeys from system to system were seldom even imagined.

One of the first men to look upon such journeys as feasible was the Russian scientist Konstantin Tsiolkovsky, who speculated about space travel both in technical articles and in stories that were less fiction than lectures put into the mouths of fictional characters. Tsiolkovsky began writing in the 1890's, though much of what he wrote was not published until later. He believed not only that other habitable solar systems exist, but that man will someday colonize them. He also suggested that the populations of different solar systems unite, and assist each other in migrating when their suns explode or become extinguished.

''Is it conceivable for one apple-tree in the infinite orchard of the Universe to bear fruit, while innumerable other trees have nothing but foliage?'' Tsiolkovsky wrote. ''Spectral analysis indicates that the substances of the Universe are the same as those of the Earth. Life also extends throughout the Universe. . . .

114

All the phases in the development of living beings can be seen on the different planets. What humanity was like several thousand years ago and what it will be like in a few million years—all this according to the theory of probability can be found in the planetary world." And he also said, "We are . . . compelled to take up the struggle against gravity, and for the utilisation of celestial space and all its wealth because of the overpopulation of our planet."

The American rocket pioneer Robert Goddard thought seriously about travel to extrasolar worlds too, although his speculations on that subject were never published. In 1918 he wrote a manuscript entitled "The Last Migration," which he enclosed within an envelope bearing a different label and placed in a friend's safe. Describing this manuscript later, he referred to its suggestions—some of which concerned expeditions "into the regions of thickly distributed stars"—as "extreme." Evidently he considered them too extreme to be made public; and in fact on the inner envelope he indicated that the contents should be read "only by an optimist."

Optimism was indeed required by those who gave attention to extrasolar planets in Goddard's time. The thought of forever-unreachable worlds was more frustrating than it had been when people had not expected science to solve all questions, and had commonly assumed that souls might visit those worlds after death. While exceptional men like Tsiolkovsky and Goddard envisioned eventual interstellar voyages, that vision was not shared by many; no conceivable channel of contact between solar systems was endorsed by science. Speculation about other worlds seemed futile.

All the same, at least some people held to the view expressed in a 1901 issue of *The Spectator:* "There is a growth in man's mental power, slow as it is, and a generation may come, and that speedily, which realizes the greatness of [the] universe as fully as some now realize that of the solar system. . . . The sense of vastness should be, and is, a stimulant. . . . Ours is a poor little planet, and we are probably low down in the hierarchy of sentient beings, but we are part of a mighty federation, and we may rise—we may rise."

PART II

The Knowledge
of the Present

As I watch the bright stars shining—think a thought of the clef
  Of the universes, and of the future.
A vast similitude interlocks all,
All spheres, grown, ungrown, small, large, suns, moons, planets,
  comets, asteroids,
All substances of the same, and all that is spiritual upon
  the same,
All distances of place, however wide,
All distances of time—all inanimate forms,
All Souls—all living bodies, though they be ever so different,
  or in different worlds,
All gaseous, watery, vegetable, mineral processes—the fishes,
  the brutes,
All men and women—me also;
All nations, colors, barbarisms, civilizations, languages;
All identities that have existed, or may exist, on this globe,
  or any globe;
All lives and deaths—all of the past, present, future;
This vast similitude spans them, and always has spann'd, and shall
  forever span them, and compactly hold them, and enclose them.

—Walt Whitman
On the Beach at Night Alone (1856)

chapter seven

But how shall mortal wing
Attempt this blue profundity of Heaven,
Unfathomable, endless of extent!
Where unknown suns to unknown systems rise,
Whose numbers who shall tell? stupendous host!
In flaming millions through the vacant hung,
Sun beyond sun, and world to world unseen. . . .
What search shall find
Their times and seasons! their appointed laws,
Peculiar! their inhabitants of life,
And of intelligence, from scale to scale
Harmonious rising and in fix'd degree;
Numberless orders, each resembling each,
Yet all diverse!

—David Mallet
The Excursion (1728)

At present—about three-quarters of the way through the twentieth century—the words above, written nearly 250 years ago, have relevance undreamed-of until quite recently. The poet who wrote them thought his questions unanswerable except in terms of imagination, as far as mortal beings were concerned. He assumed the answers were revealed only in death to souls like Sir Isaac Newton's, which in life, "From truth to truth ascending, gain'd the height of science." Step by step science has ascended to heights Newton could not have imagined. Today it is beginning to seek those answers.

In September of 1971, a group of American and Russian scientists held a conference in Soviet Armenia, at which they decided that astronomy, biology, computer science and radiophysics have reached the stage where "serious and detailed

119

investigations" of possible communications from other solar systems are warranted. It was agreed that the results might influence the whole future of man, and that the working group should be multinational.

In June of 1972, the U.S. National Academy of Sciences issued a report on the future of astronomy stating that our civilization is "within reach of one of the greatest steps in its evolution: knowledge of the existence, nature, and activities of independent civilizations in space." This report said that each passing year has seen estimates of the probability of extrasolar life increase, and declared, "More and more scientists feel that contact with other civilizations is no longer something beyond our dreams but a natural event in the history of mankind that will perhaps occur in the lifetime of many of us."

Not everyone agrees that contact is likely to be made as soon as that, or even that such contact would be desirable at man's present stage of evolution. Issues of that kind involve opinion, not scientific knowledge, and are therefore discussed in Part III of this book, "The Questions of the Future." But most scientists do believe, on valid grounds, that other civilizations must exist. One of the authors of the National Academy of Sciences report was Dr. Frank Drake, a noted astronomer who has been studying the field of interstellar communication since the time, not too many years ago, when conservative scientists thought him foolish. They do not think so any longer.

Recently Dr. Drake was interviewed by a writer for a national magazine, who asked him what the probability is of life existing elsewhere. Dr. Drake replied that the probability is 100 percent that there is life beyond our solar system. "That theory I think is almost universal," he said. "I've run into only one or two scientists who don't feel that way."

Obviously, this represents a great change from the view predominant during the era between the two world wars, the era when extrasolar worlds were considered rare. What has happened during the past quarter-century? Why have scientists returned to the beliefs of an earlier period, often without being aware that the new conviction about extrasolar civilizations is not really new? This question is less puzzling than those concerning the previous shift of opinion. Major advances in scientific knowledge have played a large role in the recent change, and those advances can be specifically defined.

In the first place, the "accidental" concept of the origin of planetary systems has been abandoned. The theory proposed by Sir James Jeans and others, which held that planets are formed as the result of a close encounter between passing stars, is no longer accepted by science. It is now known that many features of the solar system cannot be accounted for by such a theory. Moreover, in the 1940's one of the main objections to the old nebular hypothesis was found to be invalid. Until then it had been supposed that suns were composed of the same elements as Earth in approximately the same proportions; and if that had been true, condensation of planets from a solar nebula would not have fit the proven laws of physics. But the elements most abundant on Earth actually represent less than one percent of the matter in the universe. Suns and interstellar matter consist primarily of hydrogen and helium. When that was discovered, theories of the nebular type were seen to be more accurate than had been thought.

The question of how solar systems originate is far from settled. A number of different theories have been advanced, none of which are conclusive enough to be wholly accepted by astronomers, and new information is constantly being gained. But current theories do have one thing in common. They do assume that formation of planets is a natural part of stellar evolution, and that although it may not occur with all types of stars, it is in no way unusual. This means that solar systems are no longer believed to be rare. Estimates of the probable number in existence vary, but all say there must be millions in our galaxy alone.

There is, in addition, far more dramatic evidence that many extrasolar planets exist. A few such bodies have been detected through observation of the closest stars. They have not actually been seen; no telescope is powerful enough to enable planets to be seen at interstellar distances. What has been observed is the effect of the planet on the motions of its sun. Exact laws determine the motions of all heavenly bodies, laws that make it possible for these motions to be calculated with great precision.

When the observed motions differ even slightly from the calculated ones, it is known that an invisible body must be exerting gravitational influence on the star that is visible. It is also possible to calculate the mass and orbit of the invisible companion.

As far back as 1943, it was found that the star 61 Cygni has such a companion; and since then several other cases have been discovered. At first astronomers hesitated to call them planets. For one thing, the "dark companions" were much larger than any of the planets in our solar system; 61 Cygni's is about 16 times more massive than our largest planet, Jupiter. Also, 61 Cygni is a double star, which complicates matters. But in the last few years two dark bodies with approximately the same mass as Jupiter have been found in the system of Barnard's star, which is single. Calling them planets has been considered justifiable, and doing so has increased the feeling that other "dark companions" are probably planets, too. After all, the main distinction between a planet and a star is that a star shines by its own light, while a planet shines by reflected light. The trend today is to call any object too small to generate enough heat for a nuclear reaction at its core (which would give light) by the name "planet."

The most recent extrasolar planet to be discovered orbits the star Epsilon Eridani. Its finding was announced in February of 1973 by the American astronomer Peter van de Kamp, who also discovered the dark companions of Barnard's star. Dr. van de Kamp spent many years and compared hundreds of telescopic photographs showing each star in order to chart the slight "wiggle" in its motion. The observed width of this wiggle has been compared to that of a human hair seen from a mile away. A wiggle in the motion of another star, Lalande-21185, is being analyzed by Dr. Sarah Lippincott, who detected it; but although she has been working on it for thirteen years, it has not yet been possible to verify the presumed planet's mass and orbit.

All of the planet-like objects so far known are much too massive and too cold to support life of the kind known on Earth. They are not considered potential homes of extrasolar civilizations. However, it is possible that smaller planets exist in the same solar systems, planets that are closer to their suns and therefore warmer. Such planets could not be detected by present observational methods; they would not have a great enough effect on their suns' motions. Even if better techniques of observation should be developed, data on the motions would have to be collected over a long period of time for the ''wiggles'' to become apparent. So there is no hope of finding evidence of habitable planets very soon.

Nevertheless, discovering the ''dark companions'' of stars has greatly strengthened the grounds for belief in habitable solar systems. The stars found to have these companions are, of course, among the ones nearest to us, since slight variations in the motions of more distant ones would not be observable. The laws of probability make it incredible for there to be several planetary systems so close to each other if such systems are not common. This fact was one of the reasons for the final rejection of the ''accidental'' theory of the solar system's origin. The odds against even one near-collision between stars are so great that our system was thought somewhat freakish when an encounter of that sort was believed to have formed it; though statistically, the universe was even then assumed to contain others, the statistics were based upon billions of stars. The odds against four or five encounters within so few light-years of each other are for all practical purposes incalculable.

Another type of indirect evidence for the existence of many solar systems concerns the rotation of the stars. The sun, like the earth, spins on its axis; and the other stars do also. But they do not all spin at the same rate. Many of them rotate much faster than our sun, and according to the theories believed by most astronomers, fast rotation is normal in the early stages of a star's evolution. It is thought that the most probable cause of slower rotation is the transfer of part of the spinning momentum to other bodies: to the components of double or multiple star systems, to planets, or perhaps to both. If this is true, it means that slow-spinning stars, at least the single ones, must have planets. Vast numbers of such stars have been observed.

It so happens that the slow-spinning stars are similar to our sun in other ways also. Stars differ greatly in color, brightness, size and age. Through spectroscopic analysis, astronomers have divided them into classes. A star's class tells something about its type of light and heat, as well as its stability. The stars of some classes are not nearly as stable as our sun, and their energy output may not remain constant long enough for life to develop on their planets even if they have any. The stable classes of stars, however, are the very ones that rotate slowly.

This seems more than a coincidence. The science of cosmology is not yet far enough advanced to make positive statements about all the factors involved, nor is there any proof that only slow-spinning stars have habitable planets. There is no actual *proof* for any of the theories about the prevalence of planetary systems. But if a definite correlation should be found between rotation rate and the presence of planets, then there would be good grounds for believing that solar systems come into being only when suns are sufficiently stable to permit the evolution of life. Had the astronomers of the eighteenth and nineteenth centuries considered that idea, they would have interpreted it as evidence for their conviction that the purpose of a planet is habitation. Modern astronomers do not attempt to deal with the question of purpose, which cannot be discussed in scientific terms. The concept of *pattern,* however, is basic to science; and many people believe that pattern and purpose are related.

To be sure, life does not evolve on every world in every solar system; our own system gives proof of that. (The lifeless worlds may nevertheless be habitable, an issue discussed in Chapter 10.) And there is no way of knowing whether lower forms of life evolve into intelligent life in even one case per system. Still, many scientists now describe the probable number of inhabited planets with words long ago used by Giordano Bruno and by three centuries of his successors, such as "countless" and "innumerable."

These words convey more than numbers. Nearly every book or article about extrasolar life mentions figures as to how many stars there are, how many solar systems there may be, and how many planets can be assumed to exist. Often an estimate is made as to the number of habitable planets. But the figures are very approximate. For example, when it is said that there are 100 billion stars in our galaxy, this does not mean that anybody has counted 100 billion! All such estimates are based on formulas developed in accordance with particular theories, so they often do not agree. Furthermore, they do not really matter much. They are important to scientists in some cases, but they have little significance for anyone else. It is of interest to know whether the galaxy may contain mere thousands of planets or millions—beyond that, there is not a great deal of difference, as far as how one views other solar systems is concerned. Most people cannot visualize a million. And if it is said that there are a million solar systems, the number of planets calculated will differ by at least a million for every different guess as to the number of planets per system. Our solar system has nine primary planets, but there is no reason to treat that as a mathematical average.

There is only one respect in which calculations of the probable number of extrasolar worlds is of true concern, and that is in connection with the possible number of habitable ones within a reasonable distance of our sun. This involves many other factors, depending on the definition of habitability. But even the most conservative estimates make the number huge.

Some people are awed by large figures. Yet the vastness of space, and the number of suns in it, has little to do with meaning. A single race of sentient beings in addition to man is highly meaningful, for it means that man is not alone. The thought of many planets, inhabited by many species, means even more; and certainly the likelihood of contacting other civilizations is an important question. But the extent of meaning cannot be determined by arithmetic. Ten million civilizations cannot be considered a million times more meaningful than ten.

*

A single instance of extraterrestrial life would, if it were discovered, have great meaning to science as well as to people in general. Dr. Frank Drake has pointed out that such a discovery would absolutely prove that life is not a freak occurrence. "To think that there are only two abodes of life in the entire universe, each close enough to the other to be discoverable, would be absurd," he said. "If we find that there are two nearby abodes among the billions of celestial bodies, that could only mean, in terms of statistical probability, that life exists everywhere."

In past years, before biologists knew much about the origins of life, some did think that it might be a freak occurrence even if habitable planets themselves were abundant. Today, however, much more is known about biochemistry, and biologists believe that life develops wherever the right conditions are present. Not all of them believe intelligent life evolves often, but the ones who do not are a decreasing minority.

There are some, of course, who believe sentient life comes into being only as the result of a special act of God. But that belief has no bearing on the probability of its occurring frequently. The earlier chapters of this book tell how many generations of the past were sure that God must have created intelligent inhabitants for countless worlds throughout the universe. Most religious leaders of today who have written about the question feel that this is likely. It is not necessary to agree with all the theories of biochemistry to reach such a conclusion.

The people least inclined to believe in the prevalence of life were late nineteenth- and early twentieth-century scientists who did not believe in special acts of God, yet who did not have enough scientific data to explain its origin. They were the ones who had to resort to "chance" in order to account for it. Present-day biologists favor natural rather than accidental theories of origins, just as present-day astronomers do. Very few scientists who have observed the exciting discoveries of the past few decades give mere chance credit for any of the features of the cosmos (though they may speak of "chance" in the *statistical* sense, which is a different use of the word). All scientific discovery involves analysis of principles, or patterns. People with religious faith believe the patterns come from God; but those with a wholly opposite view agree that natural processes are not patternless. For instance, a Soviet scientist wrote more than fifteen years ago, "The laws of dialectical materialism state, without controversy, that life appears and evolves in different corners of the universe."

Nineteenth-century scientists had good reason to be skeptical of the idea that life could have arisen on Earth, or on any other planet, from nonliving matter. Such a hypothesis appeared to be a backward step. The former belief in "spontaneous generation," which had been held for hundreds of years, had recently been overthrown. It had been reduced to the status of a superstition; people had learned that maggots do not simply grow out of rotten meat, and that even microscopic organisms come only from parent organisms. Moreover, although there was controversy concerning the nature of the essential difference between organic and inorganic material, the concept of a sharp dividing line was thought to be firmly established. That too had been a triumph for science; many earlier thinkers, including Bruno, had thought worlds themselves were in some way animated.

Scientists in the early part of this century argued that if life had once arisen from inorganic matter, the same thing would be happening over and over, all the time. That was why many turned to the "panspermia" theory, under which primitive lifeforms were supposed to have come from space (a theory that is now being revived by a few who feel it may apply to *some* planets). What was not taken into account was the possibility that conditions on Earth were not the same billions of years ago as they are now. Modern biochemists believe that the atmosphere and oceans were different; they feel that organic molecules could have been formed from the chemical elements dissolved in the primeval seas. In fact, they have proven it experimentally. When electrical energy or radiation is applied to a mixture of those elements under sterile conditions, organic molecules do form.

This is not to say that living organisms have been created in this manner—that is, in a laboratory. Organic molecules are the building blocks of life, not life itself. Today it is known that all life on Earth is based upon extremely complex molecules of deoxyribonucleic acid, or as it is usually called, DNA. In the oceans, before life appeared on this planet, organic molecules apparently formed; and eventually they must have combined into DNA molecules, which can produce replicas of themselves. But although DNA is found in every living cell, a DNA molecule alone is not a cell; it is not actually alive. The means whereby the first cells came into being is not fully understood.

127

That they were generated somehow in what is known as the "organic soup" is a widely accepted conclusion, for all the ingredients were present. The energy needed to trigger the chemical reactions was also present, in the form of lightning and of radiation, stronger radiation than reaches Earth's surface through the atmosphere of today. But life cannot arise that way again on Earth, because once living organisms exist they absorb the organic molecules. The chemical phase of life's evolution seems to have lasted a billion years or more. When that phase was over, the new factor of life began to modify the conditions that permitted it to come into being. Long before the atmosphere had been modified by photosynthesis—the giving off of oxygen by plants—the mere presence of organisms made chemical generation of new organisms impossible.

If life can start naturally, through a chemical process, why is this not an inevitable occurrence on every planet? The answer to that is much simpler than explanation of the process. Almost all of today's scientists believe that it does take place inevitably—on every planet where the conditions are right.

Defining the conditions, however, is not so easy. The environment needed for evolution of the type of life existing on our planet is known. But so far, no other planet except the lifeless moon has been visited, and it is not possible to generalize from one case. Observation shows that the chemical composition of countless stars is similar to that of the sun. It shows that the laws of physics apply to distant regions in the same way that they apply here. Chemists and physicists therefore can make generalizations; they have studied many cases in different parts of the universe. Biologists cannot make such generalizations because they have not yet observed the life of any other world.

This is one reason why the exploration of our own solar system is vitally important to science. The discovery of life—even primitive forms of life—on Mars would yield crucial clues for the understanding of life in general. If life should be discovered on Jupiter, where the conditions are not suitable for terrestrial life, far more would be learned; and in fact, definite knowledge that there is no life at all on Jupiter would in itself tell biologists a great deal. The scientific value of space probes and future manned expeditions is not just in finding out what nearby planets are like. It lies in the collection of data needed to make judgments about the rest of the universe.

Until more information becomes available, the conditions required for evolution of life cannot be positively known. But some are considered by most scientists to be nearly indisputable. For instance, life of any form requires a source of energy, which according to present knowledge means that it can arise only on planets reasonably close to their suns. It requires more or less consistent temperatures, so it must have a planet with a fairly circular orbit, and the planet's axis must not be too sharply tilted to the plane of its orbit; otherwise the seasons would vary too much. The planet must rotate on its axis fast enough to keep the same side from always facing the sun, so that there are days and nights. And as mentioned earlier, the sun must remain stable, without significant fluctuations in light and heat, for billions of years.

An atmosphere is necessary; this demands that the heat received by the planet be neither so little that the atmosphere freezes, nor so much that it boils away. In addition, the planet's size and density determine whether it can hold an atmosphere. If the planet is too small its gravity is too low. An extremely massive planet, on the other hand, would have such high gravity that all presently conceivable organic matter would be crushed.

Life also requires elements capable of forming organic molecules, and it needs a liquid in which those elements can dissolve and mix. Terrestrial life is based on the element carbon, and, of course, on liquid water. Some biologists believe that all life in the universe is based on carbon and water, which may very well prove to be true; but the possibility of other life-chemistries cannot be ruled out without more evidence. A few elements besides carbon form long-chain molecules, and there are liquids besides water that might serve as a solvent. There has been a great deal of speculation about this. The speculation, however, is more restrained now than in earlier centuries, when scientists supposed life might be adapted to any environment whatsoever.

The more science learns about life, the more apparent it becomes that living things are not as they are simply by accident, but for very definite reasons. Carbon, for instance, is the only element that forms molecules as complex as DNA. The shapes of various creatures are not arbitrary; they seem to have evolved according to principles compatible with each other, despite the tremendous variety these principles permit. Scientists feel that the laws of physics, chemistry and biology fit together in a pattern. Not all of the pattern is known, and it cannot be, while man is confined to a single world—no doubt parts will remain obscure after many worlds have been explored. But its basic features, so far as can be determined, are the same throughout the cosmos. There is growing confidence on the part of scientists that this is as true with regard to life as it is in other respects. However different the details may be, the conditions for life fundamentally similar to ours appear to occur universally.

In the last few years, radio telescopes have detected molecules of substances essential to life in distant clouds of interstellar dust. Some are the same sort of primitive molecules from which the building blocks of life on Earth are thought to have been originally formed. The implications of this discovery are tremendous, and it is too soon to say what it signifies. One thing is clear, though: the components of life are everywhere. Most scientists are convinced that whether or not extrasolar life based on other chemistries exists, there are overwhelming odds in favor of abundant life like our own.

Of course, that does not necessarily mean that there are inhabitants of other solar systems who are humanoid in terms of appearance. In the first place, the evolution of life on a world is no guarantee that intelligent beings will ever evolve there, although few scientists feel that there is any reason why they should not do so in every environment suitable for higher life-forms. What is known of biological evolution suggests that intelligence is a characteristic always preserved and (over the course of eons) improved. It is much more basic than physical shape. Scientists are divided in their opinions about the relationship between shape and advancement. Some think the chances of humanoids developing elsewhere are fantastically low, while others believe that sentient peoples may resemble man closely in the physical as well as the mental sense. They have pointed out that there are a limited number of ways in which the needs of an evolving species can be met. Like Christian Huygens, back in 1698, some have argued that rational beings would need hands.

Most of the issues associated with the nature of extrasolar beings involve not knowledge, but questions. Such questions are discussed in Part III of this book.

*

The knowledge gained in the decades just past has caused scientists to readopt the once-firm belief that our planet is only one among innumerable inhabited worlds. It has done so largely by showing that Earth, and the life on Earth, seem not to have been accidentally formed, and that the natural laws resulting in their formation can be reasonably assumed to operate throughout the universe in the same way. Someday, people may look back on the mid-twentieth century as a period comparable to the mid-seventeenth, when it was found that the earth and celestial regions are not really different.

But people will look back on the mid-twentieth century for another reason. They will never forget the dawn of the Space Age; the period from Sputnik 1 in 1957 to Apollo 11 in 1969 will surely rank as one of the most significant times in mankind's history. Is it simply a coincidence that this period was the one in which the views of scientists toward other solar systems changed?

Probably it is not. There are many factors that might suggest a connection between the two developments. For instance, space flight aroused people's interest in the universe, and scientists are people who, like anybody else, are apt to give thought to topics of current interest. Then too, some scientists had scorned space travel in much the same way that they discounted the idea of other inhabited planets. So had many other educated writers. The following quotation comes from a magazine article published in 1934:

> There frequently appears in our city newspaper or in the popular magazines of pseudo-science a news note or fea-

ture article describing a proposed car or rocket for travel to the planets. So very persistent is this type of rumor that, ill-balanced though the dream is, the idea seems to have gained some currency that interplanetary transport cars are soon to become a reality. . . .

But let it be supposed . . . that the car has been financed and built, that the earth has been left behind, that the occupants have not been smashed up in the "hop-off," that they are liberally provided with food. . . . They might well appear to be nicely on their way, but at once arises a host of problems. . . . The question of steering is a serious one, even if the navigators retain possession of all their sense faculties. To guide a tiny rocket car unerringly through millions of miles of space toward a distant planet perhaps smaller than the home base. . . . The human mind has done some amazing things but none as remarkable in its way than that and the possibility of such a feat is more remote than the planets themselves. . . .

As perplexing as any of the others is the return trip problem. . . . Traveling at high speed, as the rocketeers propose, critical steering would be impossible and a landing could not be made at an exactly predetermined spot. If they came down on firm dry land, even though in the center of the desert or the great Siberian wilderness, it would be phenomenal and unbelievable luck. The chances are much greater that they would whirl tragically into the sea, marking the ill-fated extinction of a group whose energies might well have been directed along more rational channels.

If any of the scientists who agreed with such articles in the 1930's remembered them when, in the 1960's, they watched the Apollo recoveries on television, they may well have been set to thinking. They may have hesitated to criticize their younger colleagues who took interest in planets of other stars. The article quoted above had declared typically, "Whether there are these other bodies or not, the question of their possible inhabitants is, for earth-dwellers, a pointless and unimportant matter."

Proof of the feasibility of space travel, however, was not the major cause of science's increasing interest in extrasolar worlds. Interstellar travel is still considered impossible by some scientists, and impractical by most of the rest. Of far greater significance was the development of the radio telescope, which offers a potential channel for interstellar *communication*. To people who believe in the existence of other civilizations, the thought of actually communicating with them is the most exciting prospect imaginable.

It is also a justification for devoting effort to the study of other solar systems. Scientists cannot afford to spend time and money studying things about which they cannot hope to obtain any data. There is too much work of higher priority to be done. Furthermore, a scientist naturally wants to discover something through his work; to choose a field where he sees no chance of doing so would be much too discouraging. Today's scientists are unlike past "natural philosophers" who simply thought and wrote.

The possibility of radio communication between solar systems seems the biggest reason for the attention now given to other systems by scientists. Almost without exception, the ones interested in extrasolar worlds feel that communication—at least on a one-way basis—may sooner or later be established.

chapter eight

Beyond the bounds our staring rounds,
Across the pressing dark,
The children wise of outer skies
Look hitherward and mark
A light that shifts, a glare that drifts,
Rekindling thus and thus,
Not all forlorn, for thou hast borne
Strange tales to them of us.

> —Rudyard Kipling
> *To the True Romance* (1893)

In the year 1900 the French Academy of Sciences announced that a widow, Madame Guzman, had given 100,000 francs for a prize to be awarded to whoever first established communication with another world. During the late nineteenth century there had been quite a bit of speculation about communicating with Mars; but Madame Guzman was not thinking of Mars—she specifically excluded it, presumably because she thought communicating with Martians would be too easy. In one of his books Camille Flammarion wrote, "There is no need to despair of entering some day into communication with these unknown beings. . . . The idea . . . is no more audacious and no less scientific than the invention of spectral analysis, x-rays, or wireless telegraphy."

Early ideas about interplanetary communication concerned

visible signs such as lights or extensive geometric plantings. But in 1900 the scientist Nikola Tesla declared that during the course of experiments made in the previous year, he had detected radio signals he thought might be of extraterrestrial origin. "The feeling is constantly growing on me that I had been the first to hear the greeting of one planet to another," he said. When asked to suggest one of the great possible achievements of the next hundred years, he replied that it would probably be confirmation and interpretation of the greeting.

The hundred years are not yet over, and many scientists have begun to agree that a "greeting" may reach Earth within that period. It is unlikely that Tesla himself heard one with his primitive equipment, or that Marconi, the inventor of practical wireless telegraphy, picked up extraterrestrial signals in 1921 as he believed. Today's equipment, however, is far more sensitive—sensitive enough to detect messages over interstellar distances even if the transmissions are no more powerful than those of which our own technology is capable. The transmissions would not necessarily have to be directed to our planet; it might be possible simply to "eavesdrop." Listening has been tried, and there is a growing feeling that it should be tried on a far greater scale.

In 1932, when solar systems were still considered extremely rare, an article in the magazine *Scientific American* said:

> Radio waves represent our first tool with which it may prove possible to carry a signal across the great reaches of astronomical space. . . . If life does exist somewhere else, and it is reasonable to expect that it does, then some day someone is likely to encounter, by means of radio, an extra-terrestrial intelligence. What a sublimely dramatic moment it will be for those concerned when this first interstellar contact is made! Will it not dwarf every other dramatic incident that ever happened upon this earth?

The author of that article was thinking of ordinary radio receivers; the first radio telescopes were not built until about ten years later. The idea of conducting a deliberate search for interstellar communications was not seriously proposed until 1959, when two independent plans were put forward. One was published in the British magazine *Nature,* which is a journal for scientists and does not print articles unless they are judged to have scientific merit. The article about the feasibility of listening for messages from other solar systems was by two well-qualified scientists, Giuseppe Cocconi and Philip Morrison; and what they wrote is now famous as the first modern suggestion—at least the first public one—that an attempt should be made to receive messages from extrasolar civilizations.

Dr. Cocconi and Dr. Morrison felt advanced societies must consider our solar system a likely site for development of a civilization, and that they may "look forward patiently to the answering signals from the Sun which would make known to them that a new society has entered the community of intelligence." They gave detailed speculations about the technical aspects of the signals such societies might send, and about the best radio frequencies to monitor. "The probability of success is difficult to estimate," they concluded, "but if we never search, the chance of success is zero."

Although Dr. Cocconi and Dr. Morrison did not know it, a search project was already in the planning stages at the National Radio Astronomy Observatory at Green Bank, West Virginia. It was the idea of Dr. Frank Drake, and had been approved by the observatory's director, Otto Struve, a world-famous astronomer who had always been interested in the idea of extrasolar life. The plans for the project were not made public until after the appearance of the article in *Nature,* but later Dr. Struve wrote, "I believe that science has reached the point where it is necessary to take into account the action of intelligent beings, as well as the classical laws of physics." He was not referring to beings on Earth alone.

Dr. Drake named his plan Project Ozma, after the princess in the Oz books, describing the land of Oz as "a place very far away, difficult to reach, and populated by exotic beings." Project Ozma was actually put into operation in 1960. A large radio telescope was used to study two stars, Tau Ceti and Epsilon Eridani, both of which are about eleven light years away. (Since radio signals travel at the speed of light, this means that if any messages had been picked up, they would have been ones transmitted eleven years before.) No messages were heard. It would have been truly astonishing if they had been, for that would have meant that out of all the stars within range, the sun of a civilization more advanced than ours had been tried *first*. Such a coincidence is extremely improbable; yet a start had to be made somewhere, and the stars chosen seemed among the best candidates even then, before it was known that there is at least one planet orbiting Epsilon Eridani.

Failure to receive signals suggesting artificial origin does not prove that there is no inhabited world in Epsilon Eridani's solar system, or in Tau Ceti's, if it has one. The chance of there being a civilization so near Earth at a level close to ours is incredibly remote. Evolution of intelligent life on a planet takes several billion years; evolution of a technological civilization to the point where it can transmit radio signals takes still longer. *Homo sapiens* has existed on this planet for at least a million years and has known about radio for less than a century. Any nearby civilizations are probably either far behind man or far ahead. Those far behind cannot send messages. It may be that those far ahead do not want to, or that they use methods man has not yet discovered.

Since 1960, scientists have done a great deal of detailed speculating about extrasolar civilizations. This is their only way of forming personal judgments as to whether an effort to "listen" is likely to achieve enough to make it worthwhile. But all speculations about what other civilizations may be like are just that—speculation. No one knows anything about sentient beings other than man. Scientists do not know more than other intelligent people, and their opinions are simply opinions. Because these opinions do not represent scientific knowledge, they are discussed in Part III of this book, which is concerned with questions to be answered in the future.

Nevertheless, most scientists who take interest in the subject feel that listening for radio signals is not only worthwhile, but important. If there is not really any knowledge about other civilizations, how does science justify such a belief?

At first many scientists were opposed to Project Ozma. Some laughed at it and some thought it a terrible waste of precious hours of the radio telescope's time, hours that could have been used for other important astronomical studies. Dr. Struve wrote that it aroused both more criticism and more praise than any other recent project, and that it divided astronomers into two camps: those who were all for it and those who regarded it as "the worst evil of our generation." Dr. Frank Drake was considered by some to be seeking sensational publicity instead of data. But that has changed now; the ideas of Dr. Drake and others in his field are approved by the National Academy of Sciences.

One of the reasons is that scientists have had time to think about those ideas, and get used to them. They have had time to consider the very strong probability that intelligent life does exist on countless other worlds. When they judge this probability in statistical terms, they feel there are reasonable odds that out of millions of possible planets, at least a few may have inhabitants who think and behave in ways similar to man.

Another significant factor is scientists' recognition of the stakes. Perhaps no extrasolar civilization is transmitting signals detectable from Earth, which would in itself be valuable to know. Yet if one *is,* knowledge of its existence would be the most revolutionary discovery in the history of mankind. As Dr. Cocconi and Dr. Morrison said in their first article, "Few will deny the profound importance, practical and philosophical, which the detection of interstellar communications would have."

Not everyone feels that the impact on Earth's civilization would be good—another subject that is discussed in Part III. To seek knowledge, however, has always been one of man's most basic instincts. To fail to seek it when the means are available would be contrary to human nature. It would go against the innate desires of all who believe that truth is worth knowing, and who want to learn the truth about the universe.

There has been little opposition to a search for other civilizations on principle; most people involved think such an effort is theoretically desirable. A more controversial question is whether the potential benefits are great enough to justify the huge amount of money it would cost. Today science realizes that a few hours of searching would not serve. Unless a message is picked up accidentally, during regular astronomical observational work with radio telescopes—which is always a possibility—it would be necessary to devote at least half the time of a very large telescope to systematic monitoring of many frequencies. And although success *could* be achieved at any moment, it is more probable that long years of work would be required. That would be very expensive indeed, too expensive for existing national observatories supported by tax funds and already engaged in work of high priority.

Obviously, scientists interested in the search would like to build a new radio telescope specifically for that purpose—though even Dr. Drake feels that it should spend only half time on the project, since astronomers need stimulating work and years of full-time searching, without results, would be too discouraging and monotonous. But the prospect of obtaining money for a special telescope is slim. The National Academy of Sciences report concluded that the promise of detecting intelligent life is "now too great either to turn away from it or to wait much longer before devoting major resources to a search"; still it acknowledged that messages will probably have to be sought as a side effect of other observations, such as study of mysterious objects like quasars and pulsars.

The question of whether money should be spent on an attempt to find extrasolar civilizations is not merely a scientific one; it is related to social and philosophic issues. Some people believe money can be better used finding solutions to current problems on Earth, while others feel that older, more advanced civilizations could tell us the solutions. Some consider it a hopeless task to obtain any real information about intelligent beings unlike man, no matter how many may exist. Another viewpoint is that although contact with other solar systems may someday be achieved, astronautics is more vital to man's future and should be given priority over an effort to establish such contact. And some do believe that contact at present would be harmful.

So far, aside from Project Ozma, the principal attempts to listen for extrasolar messages have been made in the Soviet Union, where since the 1960's some radio telescope time has

139

been devoted to the job. At the joint Soviet-American conference in 1971—which was named CETI, from the initial letters of Communication with Extra-Terrestrial Intelligence, because of Tau Ceti being the nearest promising star—the delegates passed a resolution declaring that the significance of success would be so enormous that substantial worldwide expenditures would be justified. But of course, most of the delegates, both Russian and American, were scientists especially enthusiastic about interstellar communication; that was why they went to the meeting. They took care to point out that modest listening programs can be tied in with normal astronomical research at low cost, for they knew that no large project is likely to be started soon.

*

It may be wondered why scientists think they could understand messages from another solar system even if they received any. Certainly the inhabitants of another world would not communicate in English, Russian, or any other terrestrial language!

This is a complex and technical topic to which scientists have devoted a good deal of study, and the assumptions it involves are less arbitrary than those leading to the conclusion that radio signals may be waiting for detection. Although the full content of such signals might not be understood, the fact that they came from intelligent beings would almost certainly be provable. If they were deliberately transmitted by a civilization more advanced than ours for the benefit of peoples unknown to it, they could probably be decoded; and in that case they might yield considerable information.

There are, of course, a great many natural radio signals continuously reaching Earth from interstellar space; they are what radio telescopes were built to receive. Radio is simply one form of electromagnetic radiation, while the visible light received by optical telescopes is another. Stars, galaxies, and interstellar gases produce both. Astronomers are familiar with the natural signals and "cosmic noise." They would be able to distinguish coded, artificial signals, which would have more pattern.

Several times signals have been heard that sounded something like messages, but all of them were false alarms. During Project Ozma some were picked up that proved to be connected with a secret military radar test. Soviet astronomers once heard some regularly pulsed signals, but they came only in the daytime, and it was concluded that an extrasolar civilization light-years away could scarcely have chosen a schedule corresponding with daylight hours in Russia. In 1967 strange pulses of very precise regularity were called LGM's, for "Little Green Men," when they were discovered by British astronomers; but various factors showed that they were not of artificial origin. They were identified as natural phenomena and officially named pulsars.

No one supposes that radio messages from another world would be voice messages. They would be of the kind used for transmission of data from unmanned space probes, as well as for many types of information transfer on Earth: messages in binary code. Binary code is the basis of the language used by computers. It has only two characters—"1" and "0"—but a pattern of 1's and 0's can be used to convey information of unlimited complexity. Mathematical data can be expressed directly in binary numbers, and messages containing the fundamental principles of mathematics would be understood by any technological civilization in the universe, since mathematical truths do not vary from world to world.

Mathematical statements, however, would serve only to prove that the messages came from intelligent beings capable of understanding mathematics. They would not tell anything more about the civilization that sent them. Binary code can also be used to transmit nonmathematical data, but for that, it is necessary to know the code language being used. Such "languages" are normally agreed upon before an exchange of messages begins. What sort would be understandable to inhabitants of separate worlds?

The problem is not as difficult as it sounds. In fact, a solution was proposed in a 1920 issue of the *Scientific American,* when people were still hoping to establish communication with Martians. The examples given employed dots and dashes because computers had not yet been invented and binary code was not in common use, but the principle was the same. In fact, it is the same for any system of only two characters, and the authors of the article suggested that readers imagine strings of Indian beads—black beads and white ones. If the strings were placed side by side, the white beads would form a background on which properly placed black beads would show as lines, and the lines would make pictures. The article's illustrations included an outline drawing of a man formed by plotting series of dots ("white beads") and dashes ("black beads") on paper ruled into small squares.

Whether or not any of the modern scientists involved have ever happened to read the *Scientific American* for 1920, the picture idea is considered the most probable basis of interstellar communication between civilizations not known to each other. In 1961 Dr. Frank Drake mailed a message in binary code to some of his friends and asked if they could decipher it. When they arranged it with the 1's as dark squares and the 0's as blank ones, they were able to do so, although not all of the symbols included were understood by everyone, since among them were very compact representations of things such as the structure of atoms. An initial message would have to be short and compact. However, it would be merely the first step in establishing a television link between solar systems. Television works on a similar principle, though a picture transmitted across a long distance must be built up very slowly and cannot be seen without reconstruction. Pictures are much more complex than a simple pattern of black and white squares; yet in theory, their use would be feasible. And through pictures, abstract languages could be taught.

The chief difficulty in communication between solar systems is the long time lapse required between sending a message and getting an answer. If man were to receive intelligible signals from Tau Ceti or Epsilon Eridani tomorrow, and if a reply were sent at once, it would be more than twenty-two years before an answering message could be received. In addition to eleven years of travel time in each direction, time for decoding and encoding would be needed by the signalers. Yet the odds against there being a civilization only eleven light-years away are tremendous. If a message does ever come, it is more apt to be from several hundred light-years away, or still farther. No answer to our reply could reach Earth for at least twice the number of years it takes light to travel between our solar system and the other one. Civilizations evolve in the course of centuries; it is difficult to imagine them learning each others' languages—even picture languages—at such a slow rate of exchange.

Is there any hope of a faster rate? Very few scientists think so. There is no means of more rapid communication by radio, or by laser beams—another method that has been suggested. The maximum speed of electromagnetic radiation is a known constant.

Radio broadcasting on Earth began about fifty years ago. The emissions from the first weak broadcasts are still traveling outward through interstellar space. Scientists like to think that if there is a civilization twenty-five light-years away with powerful receivers, and if it is listening for evidence of a new world capable of communication, its greeting could be heard any day now. But those are two larges *ifs*. Apart from the possibility that a nearby civilization exists, the only foreseeable chance of getting advanced knowledge from an extrasolar world in the immediate future lies in intercepting messages (or perhaps an unmanned probe) from a supercivilization that transmits detailed information continuously in all directions. To be sure, many astronomers believe it may be possible to "eavesdrop" on the internal communications of other planets; but that would not yield much information—it would simply be proof of another sentient people's existence.

Yet man's civilization is still very young. As a "communicative civilization," a term used by some scientists to define one able to send and receive radio signals across interstellar distances, it is in its infancy. There is every reason to suppose that the chances of interchange with other worlds improve as a civilization matures. Moreover, the galaxy may be full of messages of a kind not yet known to us. Dr. Carl Sagan, one of the foremost scientists in the field of extraterrestrial studies, has said that Earth's people may be very much like the inhabitants of some isolated valley who communicate by drum and runner, having no idea of the international radio traffic going around, over and through them.

Forward-looking people have always had hopes for their children, their grandchildren, and even for their remote descendants. There is no way around the fact that the universe imposes limits on fulfillment of every hope *now*. Though the growing science of interstellar communication demands patience, it does appear to offer a long-range hope. Dr. Sagan suggests that because thinking only of short-term gains has proved dangerous to our civilization, the time scale of interstellar discourse may provide "a sense of historical continuity" vital for its survival.

*

Already, mankind has sent one small message into the cosmos: a message that may never be received, yet that by its very existence proves that the scientific respectability of belief in extrasolar civilizations is no longer open to doubt. It is on a plaque attached to Pioneer 10, the first spacecraft to leave our solar system.

Pioneer 10 is an unmanned probe that was launched in 1972 and, in December of 1973, sent back close-up pictures of the planet Jupiter. Its mission complete, it will pass out of the solar system into interstellar space. Its ultimate destination cannot be calculated, but it would take more than 80,000 years to reach the nearest star even if it were aimed there, which it is not. Nevertheless, scientists thought it appropriate for such an object to carry some indication of the identity of its builders. Though the chance of its entering another solar system within the lifetime of our galaxy has been computed as negligible, there is the possibility that some advanced starfaring civilization might intercept and examine it.

It is not thought at all likely that such a civilization would be hostile, and in any case, our normal radio-frequency transmissions travel far more rapidly than Pioneer 10, which could not be intercepted until the very distant future unless a starship were already close enough to be observing our world; no conceivable danger exists in revealing Earth's location. An engraved aluminum plate containing a message was therefore fastened to the probe by NASA. Combined with the probe itself, which would show the level of our technology, this simple message should tell a good deal about the planet from which it was sent.

The message was designed by Carl Sagan, his wife Linda Sagan (who was the artist) and Frank Drake. It consists of a drawing of a man and woman, plus technical symbols that specify the spacecraft's origin in time and space. These are based on a definition of units of measurement given in terms of characteristics of hydrogen atoms. Since hydrogen is the simplest and most abundant atom in the universe, they should be understandable to physicists of any civilization. There are also binary numbers defining pulsars, from which an advanced civilization could determine both our solar system's position and the epoch in which the probe was launched. At the bottom of the plate, the planets of our system are depicted, and the spacecraft is shown with its antenna aimed at Earth.

This plaque did arouse some controversy, not so much because people doubted the wisdom of calling attention to ourselves, but because a few objected to the drawing. The primary objection voiced was that the man and woman are shown without clothes. Clothes, of course, would be extremely confusing to an alien biologist, who—having never seen our species—would have no way of knowing what was clothing and what was not.

Before Pioneer 10 is examined by beings from an extrasolar world, man may already be known to them; for the odds are that interception of the probe, if it occurs at all, will take place eons hence. The significance of its message is less practical than symbolic. The designers wrote, "We do not know if the message will ever be found or decoded; but its inclusion on the Pioneer 10 spacecraft seems to us a hopeful symbol of a vigorous civilization on Earth."

*

Although modern scientists have a great deal more knowledge than those of former times, and have evidence for believing that life on planets of distant stars may be the rule rather than the exception, not all of their ideas about extrasolar life are based on evidence. They also speculate, just as people have always done.

145

Sometimes such speculations are difficult to distinguish from actual scientific theories. Most science books say a good deal about what scientists expect the civilizations of extrasolar worlds to be like. They explain the reasoning that leads to the conviction that radio signals are being sent, for instance. Often the statements sound as if they concerned established theories or even known facts.

More than a hundred years ago, one of the reviewers of William Whewell's book *Of the Plurality of Worlds* wrote as follows:

All imagined higher races are only higher *conditions* of the same race. Our power to imagine ends in this. We stand in unity, averring and affirming that such is the oneness of the whole creation that a moral and intellectual creature, whose experiences should have occurred on the most distant world imaginable in space, would, on meeting one of our earth-born, have much in common with him, of which to speak. Would not *light, weight, order, beauty, cohesion,* be substantially the same to each? And *a world* implies the presence of these. The same of mathematical truths, of moral laws, of reverence and love, of memory and hope, of believing and knowing. Despise not, therefore, our very little earth. It is manifold; and the secrets of the universe are deposited in it. It is the small key that unlocks the big chest, and the door of the vast mansion.

Most of today's scientists would agree with those words. Certainly they agree that such things as light, weight, and mathematical truths are the same on all worlds. The majority also feel that although specific moral laws, at least the interpretations of them, may differ from world to world, the basic psychology of alien beings is enough like ours for us to guess what those beings can be expected to do. There is no other basis for guessing. The only alternative would be to abandon all attempts to imagine what sort of communication may become feasible.

It is very important, however, to realize that what scientists say about extrasolar civilizations' probable actions *is* a guess. In the words of the author quoted above, *All imagined higher races are only higher conditions of the same race*: that is, of man. *Our power to imagine ends in this.* A scientist can make an educated guess as to what mankind would do if it were more advanced and had greater technological capability than at present, and he can sincerely believe that civilizations elsewhere in the universe would do the same. But he cannot claim that he *knows* what the inhabitants of other worlds would do. He may speak as if he knows because it is awkward to express his ideas in any other way, yet underneath, he and his colleagues are aware that there is absolutely no scientific proof for anyone's opinions about the most likely behavior of a civilization more highly evolved than ours.

Unfortunately, people who are not scientists do not always understand this distinction. Scientists themselves tend to forget it; when their reasoning is logical, they are apt to forget that it is based on premises not known to be facts. Even the best scientists cannot go very far beyond the premises of their era. Sir Isaac Newton formulated the law of gravitation, but despite his brilliant mind he could not have formulated the theory of relativity as Albert Einstein later did. Theories about other worlds' inhabitants are even more closely related to the assumptions of an age than theories in the realm of physics.

The main reason for this is that no observational or experimental data can yet be obtained about other inhabited worlds. But there is also another reason. The subject of other worlds is one on which non-scientists have speculated as much as scientists. In this century, until quite recently, most of the speculations known to the public concerned ideas that struck scientists as foolish; and there are still a good many of that kind. To scientists interested in extraterrestrial life, it is embarrassing. They do not want their colleagues to associate their work with the ideas often presented in sensational books and newspapers, so they are very careful to make their own speculations fit the current framework of science.

That framework will undoubtedly change in the future, as it has in the past. Certain ideas respected by scientists of former times are "foolish" according to present views, and vice versa. For example, Johann Bode, the originator of Bode's Law about

147

distances of planets from the sun, believed that the same mathematical proportions applied to the spiritual merits of their inhabitants, an idea quite common in the eighteenth and early nineteenth centuries. In other words, Martians were thought to be twice as spiritual as man because Mars is approximately twice as far from the sun as Earth. Although this notion has not been *disproven,* it is highly unlikely to prove true. Yet according to Bode's assumptions, it was plausible—and the notion of receiving pictures in code language from another solar system would not have been.

Today the idea of using mathematics to express guesses about moral qualities, as Bode did, may sound laughable. But it is not as outdated as it may seem. The latest edition of an excellent encyclopedia, in its computation — admittedly "very uncertain" — of the minimum number of technical civilizations in our galaxy, assumes arbitrarily that 1% of those that develop avoid self-annihilation in nuclear wars. And in fact, the possibility of a percentage being destroyed by nuclear war has been taken into account in quite a few estimates of the chances of picking up radio signals. Dr. Frank Drake included the parameter L in his formula, with L defined as the average lifetime of communicative civilizations; the encyclopedia's unfounded assumption that only 1% manage to escape self-destruction is employed in figuring L.

It should not be thought that such considerations are not relevant; obviously they are. Furthermore, scientists realize that the values they use in such calculations are not based on scientific data. (Dr. Drake once wrote, "It may well be that knowledge of L is itself important enough to provide a justification for a search for extraterrestrial intelligent life." He went on to suggest that in that case, perhaps L should be removed from the formula and made a goal of the search instead.) But to many people an equation seems to declare indisputable fact. They recognize that nobody on this planet has any idea how many extrasolar worlds out of a million are destroyed by nuclear war, yet when a factor of that kind is buried in a formula, they do not think to question the results of the calculation.

The speculations of modern scientists about extrasolar civilizations sound much more reasonable than the speculations of scientists like Johann Bode and Sir David Brewster. Naturally they do; they fit the beliefs of our society instead of eighteenth or nineteenth-century society. In the eighteenth and nineteenth centuries definite ideas about God's motives for creating worlds were prevalent, and scientists' picture of sentient beings on other worlds fit those ideas. In the twentieth century ideas about the progress of technology are more fundamental. Scientists therefore form pictures of highly evolved societies on the basis of reasoned opinions about the future of Earth's technology. Lately, some people have begun to have doubts about technology, and so some scientists have begun to figure in the possibility that advanced civilizations may get tired of technology and stop trying to communicate with each other.

All such speculations are in the same category. They are logical, in terms of the only data available: data concerning the past and present attitudes of man. How will they sound in the twenty-first century? In the twenty-second? How would they sound to the inhabitants of a world five thousand years ahead of ours?

If it is true that there is unity in the cosmos, and that peoples of all worlds have much in common, then man's speculations would not sound stupid to an advanced civilization. They would simply sound immature. It cannot be stated as a fact, however, that different species of sentient beings are in any way like man, for as yet there is no proof.

Is speculation useless, then? If that were the case, none of the speculations of the past would be worth anything. Bruno's ideas were entirely speculative, and he chose to be burned at the stake rather than deny them. All philosophers and scientists of the past who have made important discoveries have speculated about things that could not be proven. Without speculation, science cannot move ahead.

Scientists *must* speculate. There is nothing wrong with doing so. But speculations must not be confused with knowledge, so in this book they are described separately. The next section is entitled, ''The Questions of the Future''; but since the questions are already being asked, it is actually about questions to be *answered* in the future.

149

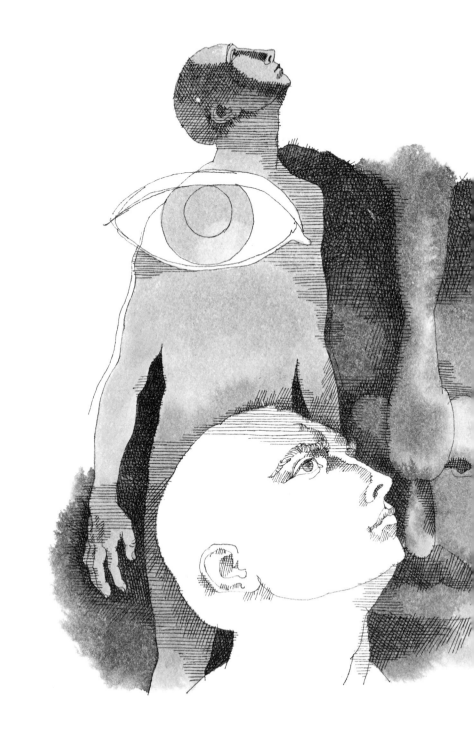

PART III

The Questions
of the Future

All the suns–are these but symbols of innumerable man,
Man or Mind that sees a shadow or the planner of the plan?
Is there evil but on earth? or pain in every peopled sphere?
Well, be grateful for the sounding watchword "evolution" here. . . .
While the silent heavens roll, and suns along their fiery way,
All their planets whirling round them, flash a million miles a day.
Many an aeon moulded earth before her highest, man, was born,
Many an aeon too may pass when earth is manless and forlorn,
Earth so huge, and yet so bounded—pools of salt, and plots of land—
Shallow skin of green and azure—chains of mountain, grains of sand!
Only That which made us meant us to be mightier by and by,
Set the sphere of all the boundless heavens within the human eye,
Sent the shadow of Himself, the boundless, through the human soul;
Boundless inward in the atom, boundless outward in the Whole.

—Alfred, Lord Tennyson
Locksley Hall Sixty Years After (1886)

chapter nine

Whate'er your nature, this is past dispute,
Far other life you live, far other tongue
You talk, far other thought, perhaps, you think,
Than man. How various are the works of God!
. . . Know you disease?
Or horrid war?—With war, this fatal hour,
Europa groans (so call we a small field,
Where kings run mad.) . . . How we wage
Self-war eternal! —Is your painful day
Of hardy conflict o'er? or, are you still
Raw candidates at school?

> —Edward Young
> "The Inhabitants of Other
> Worlds Interrogated"
> *Night Thoughts* (1745)

Speculation about the inhabitants of other worlds is nothing new; as the lines of eighteenth-century verse above clearly show, Edward Young's questions were in many respects remarkably similar to today's. Nor is it new for scientists to consider such questions. What is different today is that scientists are speculating with a practical purpose in mind. Unlike their predecessors, they expect to establish communication with extrasolar civilizations. Modern philosophers and religious leaders, too, are beginning to realize that questions about sentient beings elsewhere are not merely academic questions. Man's view of other solar systems now has evident relevance to man's future.

There has, of course, been a great deal of speculation about extrasolar civilizations in science fiction. Some authors of science fiction are as qualified to make guesses about alien civiliza-

153

tions as the scientists themselves, since no scientific data can yet be obtained in that area. An author, however, may depart from what he considers most probable for literary reasons; fiction and nonfiction are separate categories even when both contain the same type of speculation. The various speculations that follow have all been presented in nonfiction.

Today's speculations are much more diverse than those of former centuries. Most scientists agree that there is intelligent life in other solar systems, but they do not agree about the probable nature of other civilizations. There is no reason why they should. Scientific agreement is produced by evidence, and there is no evidence whatsoever in regard to the topic. An "educated guess" about it cannot be based on anything except analogy with Earth's civilization. In the seventeenth, eighteenth and nineteenth centuries scientists based their arguments for habitation of other planets mainly on analogy, and early twentieth-century scientists scorned them for it. Better grounds for judging whether planets are inhabited had been discovered. But analogy is still the only foundation for arguments about the societies of their inhabitants: a fact that is often overlooked.

Confusion sometimes arises because our languages do not yet have special words with which to describe societies of whole planets, as distinguished from different cultures on the same planet. For instance, the word "civilization" has always been applied to different cultures on Earth like Western Civilization or Chinese Civilization, and to societies like the Roman Empire. In that sense, this planet has had a number of civilizations, and some of the older ones have disappeared. But in the planetary sense man has had only one civilization that has developed in successive stages. Analogies between those stages and independent civilizations of other worlds are not exact because all the civilizations of Earth were built by human beings of the same species, whereas the sentient beings of separate worlds belong to different species. The collapse of the Roman Empire may have some bearing on the future of our present society, since the ancient Romans were ancestors of modern man; yet its only real bearing on speculation about other planets is that their civilizations may have corresponding stages. The downfall of various terrestrial societies does not tell anything about permanent halts in the evolution of entire civilized species, although such comparisons are sometimes drawn.

The word "race" causes similar problems. To many people today, race means skin color. But actually everyone on this planet belongs to the same race: our human race. There is no true analogy between relationships among people with different skin colors and relationships among the sentient races of separate planets. Whether those races are called separate *human races* depends upon one's definition of "human." If human means our species, then they cannot be. However, if human means all species with minds similar to man's, such inhabitants of other worlds are human. Some writers call them "humanoid." Unfortunately there is no uniform usage of any of these words either in nonfiction or in fiction. Even the definition of "intelligent" is open to question.

These difficulties with words complicate both the forming and sharing of ideas about extrasolar civilizations. Most speculators think it possible that some, if not all, sentient species may *not* have minds similar to man's. A few think man could never understand them. On the other hand, the majority feel that enough extraterrestrial races are "human" in terms of the way their minds work to be worth contemplating. If scientists seem to allow only for such minds, it is usually because there is no way to make meaningful statements about whatever stranger ones may exist.

But even species with minds like man's would not necessarily behave as man does, or as he might in the predictable future. In 1959, when Dr. Cocconi and Dr. Morrison wrote their article and Dr. Drake planned Project Ozma, the assumption was made that civilizations more advanced than ours would surely be trying to signal us if they were close enough. Before long, scientists began to question that assumption, as well as many others that are significant if interstellar communication is to be tried. The following ideas—all of which were proposed by scientists of high reputation—are typical of the suggestions that have been discussed.

Scientists' ideas about inhabitants of other solar systems generally concern civilizations more advanced than ours. This does not mean that they believe extrasolar beings are superior to man, as so many people of past centuries did. But our capability for interstellar communication is new, and since less advanced worlds would have none, there is no need to consider them. To be sure, some scientists do think that there are far more civilizations ahead of us than behind us, just as a matter of statistical probability. After all, according to the theories accepted by modern science, man has been civilized for mere thousands of years; and barring catastrophe, a species might remain civilized for billions.

Many are not at all sure that catastrophes are infrequent. The possibility of nuclear war wiping out some civilizations, which was discussed in the previous chapter, has received a good deal of attention. A number of speculators are of the opinion that a communicative civilization will either last only a few years, or will avert the danger and continue almost indefinitely. It is interesting, and of course very natural, that as the number of years since man's invention of the atomic bomb increases, the length of the danger period used by scientists in calculating the number of civilizations in the galaxy tends to increase. It is also natural that scientists who are deeply concerned about the danger of nuclear war have expressed the hope that communication with an advanced civilization could tell man how to avoid it.

This is not to say that all scientists are pessimists; some feel that a species able to develop a technological civilization is too intelligent *not* to avoid nuclear war. Nor is that the only peril those pessimistically inclined have thought about. It has been suggested that not only the misuse of technology, but natural calamities such as a new Ice Age, could bring about the downfall of a species that had become over-specialized. It has been said that if a superior civilization has not already made contact with us, it may be because the mortality rate of advanced species is too high for them to become abundant in the galaxy. Opinions like these, however, are not in the majority. Most of the speculations, particularly recent ones, are about the possible activities of civilizations much older than Earth's.

Science and technology on Earth has progressed rapidly even

in the past fifty years, and its rate of progress has been increasing. Things known and done today would be incomprehensible to the philosophers and scientists who contemplated other solar systems one hundred, two hundred and three hundred years ago. Yet the chances of contacting a world only three hundred years ahead of ours are less than the chances of receiving signals from one thousands of years ahead, assuming that such a world would send signals. Time, on the galactic scale, must be measured in millenia rather than centuries. How can man hope to imagine what civilizations so far beyond his level would do? Scientists know that it is not possible to guess accurately. Their objective is merely to form "working hypotheses" that can be used as guides in their search for data.

A number of basic premises strike most scientists as justifiable for this purpose. These are supported by principles found true in man's investigation of the universe and of the history of life on this planet. One such premise is that if man is not unique, then it is more reasonable to assume he is average than to suppose he is in any way exceptional. The sun is known to be an average star. Current theories of planetary formation imply that Earth is an average planet. Man *may* not be an average intelligent species, but in the absence of any information to the contrary, assuming him to be typical is the most practical course.

Present theories of evolution indicate that curiosity, efficiency and an urge to explore the environment are important to the survival of successful species. Some scientists feel that even concern for the welfare of others contributes to survival of beings that are social by nature. Man's possession of these qualities is related to his past success, and presumably to his future survival also. It has been suggested that any species that developed a technological civilization would possess them. Assumptions drawn from such a premise are not wholly arbitrary. The experience of science shows that the universe itself is not arbitrary; it has pattern, and the same patterns, wherever observation is possible, seem to apply.

Yet though man may be typical, what man will be like *in the future* is not known. Comparing man as he is today with extrasolar beings that are more advanced is therefore doubly

157

risky. Supposing that they are curious, that they do things as economically and efficiently as possible, that they care about the welfare of less highly evolved races—they still may not act in the same way as twentieth-century man would. What if they are no longer curious about the same things? What if electromagnetic radiation, the most economical and rapid form of interstellar communication of which man is aware, has been supplanted by something cheaper or faster? What if they feel that announcing their presence to less advanced worlds would not serve those worlds' best interests?

There has been a great deal of debate in technical scientific journals about the most practical types of message transmission. It has also been suggested that an advanced civilization might find it more feasible to send unmanned probes to likely stars, and that it might be more promising to hunt for signals from such a probe than for actual interstellar signals. It has been pointed out that advanced civilizations may well be already linked into a communication chain, so that Earth should expect to be contacted by the nearest one alone. An association of civilizations, it is reasoned, would be experienced in contacting new ones; methods would be used that a relatively backward world could understand.

Suggestions have been made about more ambitious things that could be done by very advanced technologies. Perhaps part of a star's energy output would be converted to a marker, a permanent beacon. Or perhaps a world could obtain the use of all the radiation in its solar system by disassembling a large uninhabited planet and distributing the matter in the form of a spherical shell around the sun; in that case no light would escape and the system would appear as a dark radiating body. Another current idea is that listening for signals from other *galaxies* might be far more efficient than checking countless stars in our own galaxy, because all the stars in a particular galaxy can be checked simultaneously, and if there is even one extremely advanced civilization there, its signals may be detectable over intergalactic distances.

Some scientists feel that higher civilizations may not be interested in contacting lower ones. Perhaps they consider us at the level of ants—biologists observe ants, but they don't try to talk to them. Perhaps they have already observed so many emerging civilizations that still another is not worth their attention. On the other hand, they may have signaled so long without getting a response from anywhere that they have become discouraged and given up. They may have given up after centuries of fruitless listening alone; transmission of planned messages is an expensive process, and a society like Earth's probably would not send such a message before receiving one. There can hardly be any to receive if all worlds are listening instead of sending.

Still more pessimistically, scientists have suggested that civilizations not destroyed by catastrophes may decline. It has been said that they may lose their curiosity, or that their people's lives may become so easy that they stop making any sort of effort. It has even been seriously proposed that they may solve all the problems there are to solve, and have no challenges left to further their evolution. What is known of evolution certainly does indicate that it depends on challenge—but it is hard to imagine that a people would solve *all* the problems. They might solve all the ones known about on Earth, but there would then be others mankind has not yet been faced with.

One speculation scientists have put forward is that contacting the civilizations of other solar systems is in itself the major challenge of highly evolved beings. In addition, it has been said that waiting for the replies—which would involve centuries of delay if civilizations are hundreds of light-years apart—may serve as a long-term goal that keeps interest in science alive and perhaps even holds societies together through continuity of purpose.

Others have suggested that civilizations eventually lose all interest in science and technology without declining: that intelligent beings whose minds are more developed than ours consider it superfluous. This issue is controversial. Many people believe that even if a sentient race developed mental powers man does not yet have, it would still need technology—although presumably it would have learned to make better use of its technology than a human race at our level. Dr. Carl Sagan, for instance, thinks it likely that societies "immensely wiser and more benign than ours are, nevertheless, more highly technological than we."

Do intelligence and technology always go together? That question cannot yet be answered, but some comments can be made about it. It depends in part on what one means by "intelligence." Some biologists feel that dolphins are as intelligent a species as man. That they have brains larger than human brains is a known fact, and recent studies have shown that they communicate among each other with complex sounds. It has been said that if scientists cannot learn to communicate with the dolphins on our own planet, they will never be able to communicate with alien beings on other planets.

But dolphins do not have a civilization. Presumably, this is because they have no hands, or anything analogous to hands, and therefore never developed any tools. Some people would say that having tools is not necessarily a characteristic of an "intelligent species" in the sense the term is used when extrasolar civilizations are discussed. There is, however, another distinction between human beings and dolphins that seems even more fundamental. Dolphins do not make any kind of visible progress. Man has changed, yet dolphins appear to have remained the same since prehistoric times.

Long ago, before anything was known about evolution, it was assumed that there was a difference between men and animals that was more than one of degree. In the scientific sense, this is now known to be untrue. Nevertheless, there are people who believe that there *is* a difference. Some of them would describe it in religious terms. But even among those who would not, some would agree with what William Whewell wrote in *Of the Plurality of Worlds:* "Animal life implies no progress in the species. Such as they are in one century, such are they in another. . . . And therefore, if we will people other planets with creatures, intelligent as man is intelligent, we must not only give to them the intelligence, but the intellectual history of the human species. They must have had their minds unfolded by steps similar to those by which the human mind has been unfolded."

To William Whewell, this somehow made it impossible to imagine intelligent beings on other planets. His critics disagreed;

they saw nothing improbable about there being progressive species on every world. None of them, however, doubted that the inhabitants of a world must *be* progressive. Scientists of today are divided. A few feel that species like dolphins, intelligent but not progressive, may be the dominant ones on some planets. Others have suggested that only one species can be dominant and progressive in a world, and that if *homo sapiens* were to disappear from Earth, another species would start progressing. Most really don't know what to say; they simply assume that on many planets at least, progressive species that build civilizations do exist. It is conceivable that the ability to develop some form of technology is more basic to progress than intelligence.

Technology does not have to be just like ours, of course. Even simple stone tools represent an initial step in technological development. Whether the steps have a necessary order, or whether they could be taken in a sequence quite different from the one followed on Earth, is a question on which there is disagreement. Could interstellar communication be perfected before the discovery of atomic energy? Some scientists think so. Some also think that Earth's technology has developed in a particularly unfortunate order, more or less by chance, and that if other forms of progress had occurred sooner man would have been spared a good many problems. In regard to this possibility, it is interesting to remember that the long-term trend in science has been to discard the convenient label ''chance'' in favor of theories that offer natural and widely applicable explanations. Only a few decades ago the formation of solar systems was thought to be an accidental occurrence.

Considerations like these are not enough to clarify the meaning of ''intelligence.'' There are further difficulties. At the opposite extreme from the nontechnological dolphins lies artificial intelligence. A number of scientists have speculated that advanced civilizations may be dominated by intelligent machines, and that interstellar communication may take place solely between one machine and another. The use of machines for this purpose has obvious advantages. There are even more advantages when it comes to actual exploration; man has already begun to send out probes such as Pioneer 10. But the speculation of scientists interested in extrasolar intelligence has gone far beyond *using* machines; some feel that there are probably civilizations composed entirely of mechanical beings whose original builders have become extinct. The Russian scientist Iosef Shklovskii, one of the most prominent men who has studied the question of life in other solar systems, wrote, ''The division of intelligent life into two categories—natural and artificial—may eventually prove to be meaningless.'' This opinion is found among both Soviet and Western writers, some of whom believe that a transition to nonbiological intelligence may be the normal course evolution of a civilization takes.

As far as ability to reason goes, there is no doubt that computers are theoretically superior to human beings. For many years machines have been man's superiors in physical abilities; they will soon excel him in dealing with information, also. Furthermore, computers can continue to advance independently; those of the future will not need to be instructed in every step by programmers. Machines alone could meet every criteria of an intelligent, progressive and technological society known to science. To most people, however, this would seem rather pointless.

It would also seem repellent, even frightening, to many. Many are repelled by the mere idea of intelligent machines. Yet they are not disturbed by cars and planes that can move faster than they can; why should they care if computers can think faster? The key, perhaps, is in the definition of ''intelligent'' and of ''think.'' These words are used to describe human minds. But if they also apply to the minds of dolphins and of computers, perhaps they are not a complete description. Perhaps human minds have other characteristics that these words do not cover.

When people picture sentient beings of other worlds, most feel instinctively that they would have more in common with those beings than with either dolphins or computers. They feel there would be a mental—or perhaps a spiritual—kinship, something ''intelligence'' by itself does not imply. If science cannot define that factor, then maybe it is something science does not yet know.

*

Practically all of the scientists who write about extra-solar civilizations agree on more than the probability of their existence. They may, and frequently do, criticize each other's theories about the nature of these civilizations and the likelihood of contacting them; but in most cases they do not question the value of such contact. Sometimes this is merely a matter of wanting to know more about the universe. In addition, however, scientists speak of tangible benefits. Many consider it obvious that mankind could learn things from other civilizations that would save centuries of scientific investigation on Earth. Moreover, some believe that if a channel of communication were set up, man would be given ready-made solutions to Earth's current problems.

A recent Soviet report speculated not only that receiving information from supercivilizations may play a leading role in man's future development, but that such a process may lead to a rapid jump of all communicative civilizations from the lowest to the highest level. "If we assume that every civilization at a certain stage of its development passes through such a learning stage," it declared, "we conclude that there will be virtually no civilizations in an intermediate stage of development or in a stage close to ours."

Not all interstellar communication enthusiasts would go quite that far; some would argue that the time-lag and other difficulties of message exchange would make the process much slower. Not all agree that supercivilizations (associations of solar systems) exist, or that they are interested in educating new members even if they do. On the whole, however, it is felt that contact would result in man's acquisition of knowledge that will be gained more gradually, and with greater effort, if Earth remains isolated.

This seems logical. It also seems advantageous; possibly, as some maintain, it is the normal course of history once a civilization develops radio telescopes of sufficient power. But there is more than one way to look at such a theory.

Social scientists have pointed out that the shock of finding that men are not the most advanced beings in the universe might be deeply disturbing. Some think it might even cause our society to disintegrate. And while most scientists have great intellectual curiosity about extrasolar civilizations, there are those who do not feel emotionally prepared to confront them. Dr. Otto Struve once told a reporter that he himself did not, and that although he believed in their existence, he hoped he would not witness their discovery in his lifetime. More recently, a noted biologist said at a symposium, "I can conceive of no nightmare as terrifying as establishing such communication with a so-called superior (or if you wish, advanced) technology in outer space. . . . One could fold the whole human enterprise—the arts, literature, science, the dignity, the worth, the meaning of man—and we would just be attached as by an umbilical cord to that 'thing out there.' "

At the same symposium an anthropologist suggested that man ought to learn to get along with his fellow men before contacting other beings, and that if more intelligent ones have observed us, they "no doubt regard us as we would regard rabies or cancer or cholera—in short, as a highly infectious disease." This view is similar to a famous statement made fifteen years ago by C.S. Lewis, the author of the Narnia stories, who also wrote nonfiction. In an article on space he said that he wondered whether "the vast astronomical distances may not be God's quarantine precautions." He was worrying not about what superior beings might do to man, but about what man might do to alien races, perhaps with the best of intentions.

Even apart from these considerations, some people have grave doubts that communication between sentient species at different levels of advancement is good. It has been said that contact with superior technology wiped out the cultures of more primitive peoples here on Earth. That analogy does not prove anything because all the peoples of Earth belong to the same species. Nevertheless, the disadvantages of such contact may be very real. For instance, the progress of *homo sapiens* might be halted by dependence on a superior civilization that meant only to help, whether "shock" was involved or not. Certainly man's own development would be altered; it would no longer proceed at its natural pace. The strongest advocates of contact admit this. They believe mankind could skip long and difficult stages of evolution, and receive solutions to problems that would otherwise require generations—perhaps centuries—to figure out. Would that really work, or would man lose something by skipping those stages?

No one knows. Without experience, man is not in a position to know. But the only way to get experience would be to make contact with an extrasolar civilization, and by then it would be too late. Is it wrong, then, to listen for signals from the stars?

Some think so. Yet it does not seem that a search for knowledge can ever be wrong; man's urge to seek is too basic, too much a part of what makes him human. What man seeks, however, he does not always find. Might that not be the case in this instance? Although man is not in a position to know whether contact would be harmful, the older and and wiser civilizations surely are. It is generally agreed that such civilizations would not wish to do any harm. So if they have found that contacting less advanced worlds prevents the inhabitants of those worlds from evolving normally, they would not send messages. They would not answer our signals even if they understood them. And they would use whatever means they have to shield their solar systems from discovery; civilizations not ready to meet them as equals would not be permitted to eavesdrop.*

One article in a recent scientific journal did suggest that superior civilizations will not be found because they do not want to be found, and have the technological ability to prevent its happening. The author of the article, however, called this the "zoo hypothesis." He felt that advanced civilizations might avoid interaction with less advanced ones in order to observe them, as man observes animals in zoos or wildlife sanctuaries; and he found the thought unpleasant. It did not occur to him that the aim of avoiding contact might be to prevent harm. Naturally, from the viewpoint of those hoping to establish interstellar radio communication, the idea of Earth being purposely barred from it is discouraging. But it is less discouraging than many other theories if premature contact is truly damaging.

* *Author's Note:* This possibility, unlike the other suggestions in this chapter, does not seem to have been considered in scientific discussions of extrasolar civilizations, at least not in any that I have seen. Readers who have wondered whether the statements about it in my novels represent my actual opinion may be interested to know that they do. However, there are complications not mentioned in the stories caused by the long time-lag that can occur between the sending of a radio message and its detection by a distant world. And like all opinions concerning the attitudes of beings more highly evolved than man, it is purely speculative and is not backed by any evidence.

165

If man does fail to pick up any artificial signals with radio telescopes, that may be the reason. Contact with superior civilizations may have to wait until ours is more mature—and what the test of maturity is, our present knowledge cannot tell us. Meanwhile, there remains the statistically small chance of communicating with a world at the same level as ours, which would be an equal exchange and therefore a safe one.

People who believe, for one reason or another, that no radio signals from advanced civilizations are likely to be detected do not necessarily believe that it is a mistake to listen for them. From the scientific standpoint, the first goal of a listening project is to find out whether or not such signals exist. It cannot be said that they do not until a thorough search for them has been made. Although negative evidence would not be as conclusive as positive evidence, it would still be valuable. At present there is no evidence at all for any hypothesis about extrasolar intelligence. Proof that existing radio telescopes cannot pick up communications from other solar systems would add to man's knowledge of the universe in one way at least; it would rule out the possibility that a nearby civilization similar to ours is trying to get in touch with us. And it would also show that help from a supercivilization will not be forthcoming in the foreseeable future.

Of course, if a supercivilization *is* waiting and *does* consider us ready for membership, as more and more scientists seem to feel, listening will find it. But there is no good reason to conclude that man's inability to make contact with a supercivilization in the present era would mean that there is no such organization in the galaxy. Nor would it mean that man will be isolated forever. Many think it would be a tragic waste to repeat what has been done before, to learn through painful steps the answers found centuries ago by other sentient beings. Yet man has already come a long way that any others who exist have traveled previously. If they are as far ahead as statistical probability suggests, they must have had means to help before now—unless no help is possible. Perhaps only by traveling the road alone can a people develop something unique and valuable to contribute to an interstellar community. Perhaps only then is the exchange of ideas between worlds of true benefit.

Knowledge, some say, is not allowed to perish; surely it must be passed on from civilization to civilization. This is hard to deny. If a sentient race were facing extinction—and many scientists believe that all do so eventually, although the issue is a debatable one—then it would undoubtedly see to it that its accumulated wisdom was preserved. But is Earth, among the youngest of communicative civilizations, yet qualified to become the heir?

*

"It is striking how space exploration leads directly to religious and philosophical questions," wrote Dr. Carl Sagan recently. He was commenting on how in thinking about space, people tend to see their own views of such questions reflected. These are no less "Questions of the Future" than scientific ones. It is still true that "religion" in its broad sense is "concern over what exists beyond the visible world," and that speculation about topics on which science has no data involves religious or philosophic speculation.

Unlike scientists of earlier centuries, modern ones do not discuss religious ideas in connection with their professional speculations about other worlds; science and religion are kept separate. However, some scientists do mention religion when they are writing about their personal beliefs instead of about their work. The astronomer Dr. Harlow Shapley, for instance, wrote, "A one-planet deity has for me little appeal."

Actually, a one-planet deity has never had appeal for anyone who was aware of other planets' existence. Since the abandonment of geocentric cosmology all who believe in God have believed that God is concerned with every planet in the universe. Nobody has claimed to have faith in a local God. Nevertheless, people of today often assume that formal religion is opposed to the idea of there being inhabited worlds in other solar systems. Those who do not belong to churches sometimes think church members disagree with the belief in extrasolar beings, and some church members worry because they think this belief is viewed with disapproval by religious leaders.

These assumptions are unfounded. It is true that the question of other worlds is frequently ignored by theologians and clergymen. But of those who have written about it, the vast majority believe that there is nothing contrary to religion in the conviction that the universe contains many sentient races. There are exceptions, of course. However, they are not associated with any particular creed. Catholic, Protestant and Jewish writers, in America and in Europe, have stated that other intelligent beings probably exist.

Not much information is available in English-language libraries about how the various religions of Eastern cultures view modern ideas concerning other solar systems. A few writers, however, have suggested that the fundamental teachings of some Eastern religions might be less affected by the concept of universal life than traditional Western beliefs. Perhaps so; yet on the other hand, many spokemen for Western religions have declared that their teachings are not affected at all by that concept. Most faiths appear to be already compatible with belief in an inhabited universe.

Unlike their predecessors of the eighteenth and nineteenth centuries, few if any Christian writers say God *must* have created sentient inhabitants for other worlds. They say simply that man does not know. In 1952 two prominent Catholic leaders published articles that were widely quoted. In the Italian paper *Civiltá Cattolica,* Father Domenico Grasso wrote, "While the presence of human beings on other heavenly bodies is not supported by a single theological argument, neither is it excluded. Catholics are free to accept it or reject it according to their own judgment." Father Francis J. Connell, dean of the School of Sacred Theology at Catholic University in Washington D.C., said, "It is well for Catholics to know that the principles of their faith are entirely reconcilable with even the most astounding possibilities regarding life on other planets."

Both these men speculated about the possible nature of alien beings. Protestant theologians have made similar speculations. For example, in response to a 1954 newspaper questionnaire answered by a number of West German scholars, one professor declared, "Only a petty faith would wish to confine God's creativity to our Earth and our kind."

The major churches have no official teachings about the spiritual status of extraterrestrial races, and members of the same denomination often disagree. Their disagreements concern many of the same issues that have been debated since the seventeenth century, but because these debates are not mentioned in history books, modern writers speak of them as if they were new. Only one issue is actually new: the question of whether men should be missionaries to other planets. A few think so, and have even suggested that interstellar radio communication might make this possible; and there are also a few who think missionaries might come to *us*. But most are strongly against the idea of missionaries in either direction. As one writer expressed it, "A believer must suppose that God will take care of his own, wherever they are."

It has been presumed that people who interpret the Bible literally might be upset by the thought of extraterrestrial life, but this is not generally true. In 1962 some sociologists took a survey of a few church members from a group they guessed would not believe in it, and they found to their surprise that most of them did. A recent book with a literal view of the Bible in relation to modern science devoted a whole chapter to the possibility of other inhabited worlds, and declared that the day life is found on another planets is "likely to be a day of triumph—showing again that man has placed too small a limit on God." The book quoted numerous Biblical passages that the author felt were references to alien beings, just as did the books of past writers like Thomas Chalmers.

Thomas Chalmers believed other worlds were inhabited by angels. Today speculation about sentient races of extrasolar worlds is clearly separated from the concept of angels. At a recent symposium, however, the dean of the Harvard Divinity School suggested that thinking about angels has prepared theologians for dealing with the topic of life beyond Earth. He considered this topic a fascinating one that may help religion avoid "the picturing of God and the universe in too naively human terms," and felt that for growing awareness of man's place in time and space "to really sink in . . . is a great achievement."

People of many faiths have such a feeling. One Jewish writer has said that someday educated man's knowledge of terrestrial affairs may be "merely the ABC of his 'higher' or extra-terrestrial or multi-global knowledge." Another, Rabbi Norman Lamm, believes the discovery of fellow intelligent creatures elsewhere in the universe will deepen our appreciation of the mysteries of God. God's goodness and providence, he wrote, "are not limited to, but certainly include, one small planet on the fringes of the Milky Way."

The Protestant theologian Paul Tillich has written that ignorance and prejudice should not prevent our thoughts from transcending our earth and our history and even our own creeds. Questions about beings of other worlds are not just theory, he said. They are important to every man's understanding of himself as a human being, not only for Christians but for all who believe in the meaning of history and the significance of human life.

Today, of course, many people have no formal religion, and some are adherents of philosophies that hold religion to be obsolete. In the Soviet Union, for example, the official philosophy is dialectical materialism, which rejects belief in God. Throughout the world there are quite a few who believe neither in God nor in dialectical materialism; they have beliefs of their own. Obviously, there are a great many important things about which people of such widely differing viewpoints will never be able to agree. What is remarkable is that most of them *do* agree in their attitude toward extrasolar worlds—that is, if they have given any thought to extrasolar worlds at all.

They do not agree about what the inhabitants of such worlds are like. They do not agree about whether it would be good for man to meet extraterrestrial beings at the present time. But the divisions of opinion on these issues are not split according to nationality or creed. It cannot be said that Americans have one view of extrasolar planets and Russians another, or that believers in God have an opposite view from unbelievers. Naturally, any man is likely to think that advanced civilizations are run the way he thinks Earth's should be run; philosophy does have some bearing on that type of speculation. But as far as a frame of mind that includes myriad forms of intelligent life is concerned, the members of our human race seem to be potentially in accord.

This frame of mind is sometimes called a cosmic view, one that encompasses the whole universe instead of our small planet alone. If Earth's population were polled, it would be found that most people are not aware of the universe and have never stopped to consider any worlds besides this one. Some have considered the idea simply as fantasy. But those who have considered it seriously have much in common, whatever their conflicts in regard to terrestrial affairs. They do not imagine Earthmen trying to conquer inhabited planets, for instance. They rarely picture aliens as hostile beings who would try to conquer Earth. And they certainly think of mankind as a single family in relation to other sentient races. In the cosmic sense, partitions based on color or custom or region do not matter.

Yet most envision a unity even higher than unity of mankind. C.S. Lewis, fearing that some men might want to exploit extraterrestrial beings, wrote, ''Our loyalty is due not to our species but to God. . . . It is spiritual, not biological, kinship that counts.'' A person whose outlook is not religious would use different words, but the underlying thought is widely shared.

chapter ten

> . . .The worlds
> We were approaching . . . some displaying
> Enormous liquid plains, and some begirt
> With luminous belts, and floating moons which took
> Like them the features of fair earth. . . . I
> Had deemed them rather the bright populace
> Of some all unimaginable heaven
> Than things to be inhabited in themselves,
> But that on drawing near them I beheld
> Their swelling into palpable immensity
> Of matter, which seemed made for life to dwell on.
>
> —George Gordon, Lord Byron
> *Cain* (1821)

Some people wonder why, if extrasolar civilizations are presumed to exist, science is concentrating its attention on communicating with them by radio. After all, this is the Space Age. For a long time travel between solar systems has been commonplace in fiction, and though many have scoffed at such fiction as fantasy, not long ago they were scoffing at stories about travel to the moon. Moreover, the speculations about advanced civilizations now appearing in respected scientific journals seem no less fantastic than the idea of interstellar flight.

To scientists, however, interstellar travel is not the simple, inevitable possibility it appears to be. It involves such serious problems that some do not consider it possible at all. Others feel that although it may, for a very advanced civilization, be possible, it is not practical enough to be worthwhile. The reasoning of the majority is as follows: radio communication is known to be feasible, and the study of how extrasolar civilizations might use it is therefore justified. Interstellar travel is not known to be feasible, so science cannot accomplish anything by considering it at the present time. Even the most ardent space exploration enthusiasts know that starships cannot be built in this century, and perhaps not for several centuries to come.

Be that as it may, questions of great importance to anyone interested in other solar systems are, "Can man ever visit them?" and, "Have their people ever visited Earth?"

The only answer that can now be given to the second question is that no one really knows. This question has received much publicity—too much. People with dubious qualifications have claimed to be able to answer it; news media have treated it both as a sensation and as a joke; spokesmen for each side have been carried away by emotional fervor. As a result, reputable scientists have often been reluctant to make any comment on it, except maybe to say that the whole concept of "UFO's" is ridiculous.

In recent years a number of scientists have come forward to say that it is not ridiculous, and that it should be investigated. These scientists agree that there is absolutely no evidence that any UFO's are of extraterrestrial origin. They also agree that there is no proof for the idea of alien astronauts having come to Earth in the past. Still, they recognize that there is no proof that ships from another solar system have *not* visited our planet. The issue is highly controversial.

When a qualified scientist says that it is not impossible for alien starships to exist, it should not be thought that he is saying their presence is likely. Dr. Carl Sagan, in a recent book about the UFO question published by Cornell University, pointed out that according to current estimates of the possible number of advanced civilizations in the galaxy, they would each have to launch an average of ten thousand starships a year for it to be statistically probable that even one ship per year would visit Earth. He mentioned a similar calculation made by the scientist Hong-Yee Chiu, which shows that the amount of metal required to build all those starships would be equal to the total mass of metallic elements in half a million stars. As Dr. Sagan admitted, both these calculations involve some debatable assumptions; but they do illustrate the fact that existence of starfaring civilizations does not in itself make it likely that UFO's are alien ships.

Dr. Sagan himself believes that there is intelligent life in other solar systems. He coauthored a book about it with the Russian scientist Iosef Shklovskii, and he has studied speculations about extrasolar civilizations—including the idea of their having contacted man in the distant past—in great detail. He was codesigner of the Pioneer 10 plaque, which he would scarcely have bothered with if he had not thought there was a remote chance of a starship someday intercepting Pioneer 10. Yet none of these things mean he thinks that starships have been seen in our skies, or that real indications of past visits have been found.

Before a congressional committee in 1968, Dr. Sagan said, "If we are being visited by representatives of extraterrestrial life to just stick our heads in the sand would be a very bad policy, I think. On the other hand, to mount a major effort to investigate these things I think requires some harder evidence than is now at hand." He went on to say that he believed more could be learned about extraterrestrial life from NASA's unmanned planetary probes and from radio astronomy.

Another thing he mentioned to the committee was that some people want so much to believe in UFO's that their judgment is affected by their emotions. Some, he said, feel that "things are so bad down here, maybe somebody from up there will come and save us from ourselves." At the same meeting Dr. J. Allen Hynek put it this way:

> From the very start there have been psychically unbalanced individuals and pseudoreligious cultists groups—and they persist in force today—who found in the UFO picture an opportunity to further their own fanciful cosmic and religious beliefs and who find solace and hope in the pious belief that UFO's carry kindly space brothers whose sole aim is a mission of salvation. Such people "couldn't care less" about documentation, scientific study, and careful critical consideration. . . . The "true believers" I have just referred to are rarely the ones who make UFO reports.

Their beliefs do not need factual support. The reporters of the truly baffling UFO's, on the other hand, are most frequently disinterested or even skeptical people.

Neither Dr. Sagan nor Dr. Hynek was referring to members of recognized religious groups; although many church leaders believe in the probable existence of extrasolar life, they do not claim to have special knowledge that emissaries from some other world are trying to save ours. Many "UFO cultists" do claim this. Some claim to have met alien beings, to have traveled in their ships, and even to be followers of the aliens' religions. Statements have been made about relationships between extraterrestrial religions and ours that seem blasphemous to some people and laughable to others. This situation is extremely unfortunate for a number of reasons. In the first place, it has caused the general public to class all discussion of UFO's as "lunatic fringe." Worse, it has caused uninformed people to assume that any kind of research dealing with extraterrestrial civilizations is in the same category.

There is still another danger. As Dr. Sagan has written, "The expectation that we are going to be saved from ourselves by some miraculous interstellar intervention works against the necessity for us to solve our own problems." That is certainly true. In fairness, it should be said that the same criticism could be applied to the view of astronomers who seem convinced that man is going to receive the mature knowledge of an advanced supercivilization by way of radio messages.

Dr. Hynek feels that more investigation of UFO's is definitely needed, and that not all sightings have been adequately accounted for. He told the congressional committee that since Unidentified Flying Objects, by definition, are phenomena that cannot be explained in conventional scientific terms, things like balloons, meteors and satellite re-entries—sometimes mistaken for UFO's—belong in the category of *identified* flying objects. The vast majority of reported sightings must be considered identified; no one doubts that. Many can also be explained by "mass hysteria" or unreliability of individual witnesses, often sincere witnesses who are not experienced enough to make careful observations and describe accurately what they have observed. The scientific disagreement comes over whether *all* sightings can be explained in such ways. Some authorities say no, while others say yes.

To conclude that truly unidentified objects are space vehicles from another solar system, it would be necessary to assume much more than the existence of extrasolar life and the possibility of interstellar travel. For instance, a question frequently asked is why the aliens, if there are any here, do not make contact with government officials. That can be fairly easily answered. It has been suggested that either our species is too primitive to negotiate with, or the watchers do not wish to interfere with our civilization. (The latter possibility, surprisingly, has been mentioned by scientists in this connection, although not in connection with radio communication—see the note on page 165.) A rather harder thing to explain is why, if they want to avoid contact, they allow themselves to be seen. Any technology capable of building starships ought to be able to shield those ships from detection, at least under conditions like those the most reliable reports have described. Reasons why they might purposely show themselves can be proposed; but all such reasons involve assumptions not supported by data.

Many, many books have been written about UFO's; most of them, even those that do not represent deliberate hoaxes or the opinions of small pseudoreligious cults, are full of material that is irrelevant. Scientific evidence concerning the probable existence of other inhabited planets is irrelevant; it would have bearing only if it showed that the probability was small. If there were no such planets, then obviously they could not be the source of flying objects. But evidence that there are many worlds does not imply that mysterious objects have come from there. Evidence that unexplained flying objects have been seen does not imply it either; there are other unexplained phenomena in the world.

To be sure, it is hard to think of another explanation for UFO's that are actually unidentifiable. Such logic, however, is the same as the logic used by eighteenth and nineteenth-century people who believed that *all* planets *must* be inhabited because they could not think of any other reason for their existence. They, like today's UFO enthusiasts, failed to consider the possibility of explanations beyond their imagination. Their arguments did not prove conclusive. Nevertheless, when the time was ripe, advances in scientific theory showed that their convictions about habitable worlds probably did contain aspects of truth—and that too could turn out to be a parallel case.

*

Putting aside the question of whether beings from worlds of other stars have ever come here, there remains the broader and more vital question of whether interstellar travel is possible. To say that it is not would mean that Earth has had no alien visitors and never will; but it would also mean that mankind can never go beyond the limits of this solar system, an idea much more difficult to believe. There are plenty of conceivable explanations for a lack of ambassadors from other worlds to ours, even if starships are presumed to be as common in reality as they are in fiction. However, cosmic-minded people generally feel sure that each sentient species eventually travels somewhere.

Some scientists do contend that flight from star to star does not occur. The author of one well-known recent article stated that his personal conclusion was that "space travel, even in the most distant future, will be confined completely to our own planetary system, and a similar conclusion will hold for any other civilization, no matter how advanced it may be." In a lecture that has become famous, another scientist, a physicist from Harvard University, said that "all this stuff" about space travel outside our solar system "belongs back where it came from, on the cereal box." These were not idle remarks; they were preceded by discussions of well-founded technical considerations concerning certain theories of rocket propulsion. But not all scientists agree with them.

Furthermore, the assumption that the idea of starships originated in the "cereal box" or comic strip type of science fiction—or in any type of science fiction, for that matter—is erroneous. Flight between suns was seriously proposed in nonfiction when fictional spaceships had gone no farther than Mars and

177

Jupiter. As far back as 1872, the author of a widely read British book wrote that a time would come when science would transform men's bodies "by means which we cannot conjecture. And then," he continued. "the earth being small, mankind will migrate into space, and will cross the airless Saharas which separate planet from planet, and sun from sun. The earth will become a Holy Land which will be visited by pilgrims from all quarters of the universe." No more detail was given, and the brief comment may not have been noticed since the book consisted mainly of controversial religious and political assertions. But as has already been mentioned, both Robert Goddard and Konstantin Tsiolkovsky wrote seriously about interstellar travel in the early twentieth century; and no doubt there were others in various countries.

Goddard, in his unpublished manuscript "The Last Migration," speculated about the use of atomic energy and solar energy by starships. He also discussed the now-familiar concept of "frozen sleep" for the passengers—a suggestion he had first written in his journal in 1905.

Tsiolkovsky's best-known statement is, "The earth is the cradle of humanity, but mankind cannot live in the cradle forever." This has been familiar to Russian schoolchildren since the year of Sputnik I, which was the centennial of his birth; and it is applicable to exploration of our own solar system. But Tsiolkovsky also wrote, "In all likelihood, the better part of humanity will never perish but will move from sun to sun as each one dies out in succession."

The interest of H.G. Wells in space travel is usually associated with his science fiction. Yet he concluded his two-volume history of man, published in 1920, with these words: "Life . . . will presently stand upon this earth as upon a footstool, and stretch out its realm amidst the stars." The term "stars," to be sure, is sometimes used loosely, especially in connection with conquering space; it can cover planets as well as suns and does not always refer to interstellar flight. It nevertheless suggests that a person thinks of space as including more than one small solar system. To anyone with enthusiasm for space travel, this outlook seems natural and indisputable. Why should there be any doubt about someday building starships?

Once people opposed trains because they thought the speed would be dangerous. Later, they ridiculed the idea of flying; an often-repeated tale tells of a little old lady who disapproved of planes because "men should travel on trains as God intended them to." Supersonic aircraft were not developed until after World War II, and it was considered a major advance that many had thought would never come. As for spaceships, the quotation on page 131 is a sample of how some intelligent people of the 1930's viewed them, and much more recently there were some who were surprised that Apollo 8 really got to the moon. Starships seem a logical future step.

But it is not simply a larger step. It is one of a very different kind, so different that scientists who question its feasibility are also supported by logic.

Man could, without doubt, send a spacecraft out of this solar system; Pioneer 10 is already on its way. That capability is not enough. Interstellar travel demands not only the power to leave, but the power to arrive somewhere in a reasonable length of time. There were never any basic scientific theories that said nothing could go faster than a train, or that a plane could not go faster than sound, or that a spaceship could not reach the velocity necessary to escape Earth's gravity. There were merely engineering difficulties—it took time to invent machines that could do what needed doing. In some cases new concepts, not previously imagined, had to be developed: for example, one objection to space travel was that even if someone invented a spaceship there would be no way to steer it, an objection that could not have been overcome without computers. Yet the invention of computers was not judged impossible in theory once the idea for them arose. With starships, the problems are more fundamental.

The nearest star is more than four light-years away. Tau Ceti and Epsilon Eridani are each about eleven light-years away. To do very much interstellar exploring, man would have to go farther; the galaxy is almost one hundred thousand light-years in diameter. In other words, interstellar travel within our galaxy would mean trips ranging from approximately five years' to a hundred thousand years' duration, one way, *if* the ship could go nearly as fast as light for the entire distance. But there is no presently known energy source that could enable a ship to attain speeds approaching that of light. As far as the distant future is concerned, it would be rash to say that such speeds are not possible, although some experts *have* said so. Assuming the discovery of new forms of propulsion, however, does not get rid of the limit imposed by the speed of light itself.

This is a theoretical limit, not one dependent on invention. According to the underlying theories of modern physics, the speed of light cannot be reached by matter, let alone exceeded. It is not a question of man's inability to develop more powerful rockets. It involves the mathematical foundations of Einstein's Theory of Relativity. The equations of that theory show that *infinite* power would be needed to accelerate an object to the speed of light, which means that if all the energy in the universe were harnessed to drive a single ship, it would still be insufficient. Speeds just under that of light are theoretically attainable; higher speeds are not. To be sure, Einstein was not omniscient; perhaps some future physicist will develop a theory surpassing his. But it will have to be a theory that explains the experimental evidence for the Theory of Relativity equally well, and there is a great deal of evidence to be explained. All the work that has been done in nuclear physics is based on Einstein's theory; that work could not have been successful if the theory were not true at least in regard to everything that lies within man's experience.

Most scientists state positively that no ship can ever go faster than light. A few feel that a future theory, as yet inconceivable, may alter our view of the physical universe. Science fiction writers, of course, have presented numerous ideas concerning faster-than-light travel; but these have no real scientific validity—any author who thought of one that has would stop writing stories and become a world-famous physicist. Many physicists have tried to find a way around the limit, and so far no way has appeared. In terms of present knowledge only three potential forms of interstellar travel offer hope.

The first is "generation travel," a concept under which a large self-contained starship—or maybe a converted asteroid—would set out for another solar system, not expecting to arrive within the

180

lifespan of the original passengers. Children would be born, live and die without setting foot on any planet, and would pass on their goal to children of their own. In time, the descendants of the people who had left Earth would reach the destination. This idea does not depend on velocity near the speed of light, and it does not violate any known principles of science, though it would demand engineering advances greater than can occur in this century. Probably there would be volunteers for the journey. Whether they would succeed in carrying out the plan is more questionable; that could be determined only by trying it.

Another idea often discussed is "suspended animation" or "frozen sleep." Scientists believe it may become possible to lower the temperature of the human body so that people can sleep for years, perhaps even for centuries, without aging. This would permit passengers to make very long interstellar trips, and it would not require the ship to travel near the speed of light, either.

If a ship did approach that speed, a new factor would enter the picture: the relativistic "time dilation." The Theory of Relativity shows that the pace of time changes as an object approaches the velocity of light. One minute becomes equal to many "normal" minutes, and much less time would elapse on board the ship than on Earth during the journey. Hard though this is to explain, and to imagine, there is experimental proof for it obtained through the study of subatomic particles. Many books discuss its application to interstellar travel in detail. For example, Dr. Wernher von Braun has described a starship traveling at a top speed of 99.9998 percent of the speed of light; in crossing a distance of a thousand light-years, 1,000 years would be measured on Earth, but this would be only 13.2 years in the lives of the astronauts. If they returned immediately, they would be less than 27 years older than when they left, though 2,000 years would have passed during their absence. Most people find such a thought incredible, but scientists agree almost unanimously that it is true. Dr. von Braun suggests that our difficulty in accepting it is similar to the difficulty men of earlier eras had in accepting the idea of "upside down" continents.

There is one important difference, however. When men did travel to the other side of the world, they returned and told their contemporaries that they had not fallen off the bottom. A man who traveled to a distant star in "dilated" time would return to a society hundreds of years more advanced than the one into which he had been born. No one would have heard from him in the meantime; radio messages, limited to the speed of light, would not arrive much sooner than he did. As far as *Earth* was concerned, the elapsed time of double the distance in light-years would not be affected by the time dilation. Some scientists feel that time dilation will solve the problem of travel between the stars. It very well may, if the goal is for people of the future to get from one solar system to another and come back alive. Goals involving the development of mankind's civilization are not so easily fulfilled.

Just what is the goal of traveling to other solar systems? One of the two scientists quoted earlier who consider such travel unfeasible said, "The only goal which may be important enough to justify the immense effort needed for interstellar space travel appears to be the search for other intelligent beings." The other said, "The notion that you have to *go* there seems to me childish." Both pointed out that radio communication with other civilizations would be just as fast and a lot cheaper, which without faster-than-light travel is true. The point might also be made that although the President of the United States has a telephone in his office, he nevertheless travels abroad to confer with the heads of other nations; still, that kind of journey is not difficult. It is perhaps safe to say that if the search for other intelligent beings were the *only* goal of interstellar flight, man would not make the effort.

Most people, however, can think of other goals. An obvious one is man's innate desire to explore. This may be a childish feeling; our human race is not yet mature enough to judge—but if past experience is any guide, it is a desire that has led to much progress. Since many of this era still feel it, what evidence is there that it should be outgrown now any more at the time of Columbus?

In 1904 a reviewer of Alfred Russel Wallace's book *Man's Place in the Universe,* referring to the belief in plurality of worlds held by great scientists of the past, wrote: "That such men entertained a theory for which they could not adduce a scientific reason indicates more on the side of its probability than any amount of scientific improbability could weigh against it. It revealed an unconscious tendency of the human mind to lean to that side of the question." Unconscious tendencies shared by large numbers of creative people usually do prove fruitful. Today, many *want* to go to the stars.

One woman's comments on Wallace's book ended the discussion of habitable worlds this way:

> Demonstrative evidence on the point is not at hand, and cannot be looked for. Arguments . . . are futile. They rest on arbitrary assumptions. Our minds are inadequate to grasp the vastness of creative design; yet common sense obliges us to admit that what is inconceivable to us may nevertheless really exist. All that we are quite certain of regarding our place in the Cosmos is that the genus Homo . . . is earthbound. No second island in space is attainable by him in his present condition. His habitation begins to seem inconveniently narrow; but there is small chance of adding to it by annexation—there are no more worlds for him to conquer.

By "present condition" that author meant life as distinguished from life after death; she could not, in 1904, envision any kind of space travel as an actual possibility. Her words sound rather unhappy.

Why do men and women feel strongly about other worlds, other suns? If it were just because they thought it might be fun to go there, this emotion would indeed be childish; yet it is not confined to children. It is felt by adults in every region of this planet who know perfectly well that they have no personal chance of going anywhere in space. It was felt by Bruno in the sixteenth century and by increasing numbers in succeeding ages. The landing of Apollo 11 brought response from people of many countries, some of whom had never paid any attention to astronomy before. Not everyone shares the feeling, but no one can deny that it is widespread.

Some of those who have pondered the question believe that the desire to go to other worlds is a human instinct, related to man's evolution. They believe it is necessary to the survival of a sentient race: ours, and that of all others inhabiting the universe.

*

In our time it has become evident that the population of Earth cannot continue to grow indefinitely. This problem is so frequently discussed that it needs no elaboration. Many people are convinced that the only long-range permanent solution to it is the colonization of uninhabited planets: first the suitable ones in our own solar system, but eventually, extrasolar worlds as well.

To be sure, there are also many people who disagree with this view. It has often been maintained that colonization of other worlds would not solve Earth's population problem. Figures have been presented to show that spaceships could not possibly carry away people fast enough to keep up with the rate of increase. For example, to hold the population of Earth constant at the 1969 rate, almost 190,000 people per day would have to emigrate. It is very true that such a plan would not be practical; no one who has thought the matter through claims that it would. Population growth on Earth will have to be slowed down much sooner than colonies can be established in any case, and eventually it will have to stop. The idea of colonization is not to get rid of extra people born on Earth by sending them somewhere else. It is to provide new lands where mankind—our human race—can continue to grow and evolve.

But, some argue, if Earth's population were stabilized, why would there still be a problem? What difference would colonization make if the terrestrial birth rate has to be controlled anyway? Those who consider colonies essential see a big difference; they believe it is contrary to nature for the population of a progressive species to be completely stabilized. Some feel that it is impossible—that the biological instinct toward growth is stronger than conscious reasoning based on man's limited knowledge, and that without colonies, despite controls there would ultimately be overpopulation, followed by a sharp drop caused by starvation or war. Others think that it is possible to achieve stabilization, but that if this should happen all types of progress would stop, and man would slip backward into decadence. Either way, they believe continued evolution of man demands ceaseless expansion.

People who feel this way are not confined to followers of any particular philosphy. On the contrary, they are found among those whose opinions conflict sharply in other respects. To give two extremes, some Christians believe that the Bible's command, "Be fruitful and multiply," is a law of God that must be obeyed literally; while dialectical materialists have traditionally held that infinity of the universe, and a corresponding infinite potential for growth and development in man, is a law of nature. A Russian scientist, Igor Zabelin, has suggested that the population explosion is man's instinctive preparation for resettlement on other planets. One does not have to agree with any of these specific ideas to believe that unlimited expansion of our human race (and also, of course, of whatever other sentient races there may be) is a basic cosmic principle.

Social scientists and others, including some of widely assorted viewpoints, have observed that the exploration of space is the only outlet left for man's pioneering and aggressive impulses. That the conquest of space might serve as a substitute for war is a common argument for exploring our solar system. Speculatively, it is also possible to argue that man's aggressive impulses are an instinctive preparation for conquering space. The length of his recorded history is only a tiny fraction of the evolutionary time scale, compared to what came before and what, in the judgment of scientists, may be yet to come. Two things are sure: man has entered space, and he does not want any more conquering of territory to be done on his home world.

At present there is no evidence for the arguments in favor of expansion; only time can show whether they are valid. But if they do prove to be true, travel within our solar system will not be enough to ensure mankind's survival. In due course, it will be necessary to travel to other suns.

A further argument for interstellar migration is that without it, our whole species could be wiped out by a single catastrophe. Or, in the very distant future, man's extinction would inevitably occur

185

when our sun becomes unstable. This will not happen for billions of years; it is not an immediate danger, and people therefore feel that it has little significance here and now. The idea, however, does affect one's outlook toward the universe. Do all sentient species ultimately die? Scientists calculating the number in the galaxy often assume that they do. The life-span of stars is known to be finite. If interstellar travel is impossible, the life-span of a civilization cannot exceed that of its mother star. Perhaps that does not matter; yet many people care deeply about the fate of their remote descendants.

Considerations like these raise questions that are unanswerable. Philosophers ponder them, but they cannot resolve them—at least not in this era, and probably not for many eras to come. One such question concerns the relationship between individual people and mankind as a whole. Some people believe that mankind is like an organism: that in a further stage of evolution, it will *be* a single organism. Just as single-cell life forms evolved into multicellular forms, they argue, species composed of sentient individuals evolve into larger entities. Others believe that individual beings always remain of primary importance, and that in highly evolved civilizations they cooperate without becoming mere parts of some "group mind." This issue is not as clear-cut as it sometimes seems to be. People who are convinced of the importance of individuals nevertheless usually consider the future of mankind more important than their personal affairs, and often choose to make sacrifices for mankind's benefit. Neither they nor advocates of the other hypothesis can explain why.

Perhaps this question sounds too abstract to worry about. So far it has been of interest mainly to philosophers—yet before the time of Giordano Bruno the question of whether there could be more than one world was discussed only by philosophers, too. Shortly after his time the invention of the telescope changed things. The invention of starships would bring about an even greater change. Theories about the future evolution of man would no longer be just abstractions.

The only kinds of interstellar travel scientists can now foresee involve *one-way* travel, at least from the standpoint of people remaining on Earth. Colonists of each new extrasolar world would

186

be completely independent, and any messages they sent back would not be received until long years after their departure. Members of crews kept young by "time dilation" could return themselves, but only to a society they would scarcely recognize. The generation that built a starship might never hear of its fate. Under those conditions, what would "mankind as a whole" mean? Our species would spread from star to star, but there would be no real communication. Earth's society would not be entirely "closed" because adventurous people, and people who wanted large families, could leave; still there would be no interaction between the new worlds and the old. What would happen to Earth? Would the *idea* of expansion alone save it, or would the home solar system's civilization decline, to be replaced by the separate ones of countless colonies that could never unite?

There are no answers now. Science fiction often speculates about such problems, and there is also speculation in nonfiction; but our century has no data to work with. Some scientists think answers could come through contact with civilizations more advanced than ours. Barring that, mankind will have to learn through experience. It is clear, however, that a means of *two-way* travel —faster-than-light travel—would be more than a mere convenience. This is one reason why authors of stories so frequently assume it exists, and why some people maintain their faith that it does indeed exist despite apparent mathematical proof to the contrary.

Very recently a few scientists have begun to discuss conjectures about "short cuts" through space and time similar to those assumed in stories. According to modern cosmology, the universe probably contains things called "black holes"—dying stars with such powerful gravitational fields that not even light can escape from them. Since they give off no light, these stars are invisible; but astronomers have good reason to suppose that they exist. Not much is known about them, but it has been suggested that if a spaceship entered a "black hole" it might emerge in some remote part of the universe, which would in effect be crossing the distance faster than light could travel. Dr. Carl Sagan thinks it conceivable that extremely advanced civilizations might have "black hole rapid-transit systems," though he is careful to point out that this is "sheerest speculation" without real basis in scientific theory. At present it is a purely imaginative idea; people aware of the universe find it hard *not* to imagine that some means of rapid interchange between solar systems will eventually appear.

With or without faster-than-light travel, if man *can* go to the stars he undoubtedly will. The dream of doing so is too powerful, too closely tied to the basic drives of human nature, to be abandoned by everyone, though some may call it foolish. The establishment of extrasolar colonies should not in itself be difficult, for there will first be colonies in our own solar system. Suitable planets in other systems are likely to be plentiful. Dr. Stephen Dole, in his book *Habitable Planets for Man*, estimated that there may be about fifty within a hundred light-years of Earth, and he was counting only those where people could live in the natural environment.

Some of those planets, however, may be already occupied. It goes without saying that people who favor the colonization of other solar systems do not suggest that man should establish outposts in *inhabited* systems. This is more than a matter of not taking over the home planet of a sentient species that has evolved there. If expansion from world to world is the normal course of evolution, an intelligent race that has not already colonized its entire solar system will someday need to do so; alien colonists must leave all its planets alone. Moreover, it is likely that sooner or later man will encounter colonists of other starfaring races, and their new worlds must not be touched either.

This seems to be a quite serious restriction, especially since biologists feel that life will evolve wherever the right conditions exist. But actually, according to statistics, it should not be. If present theories are right, there are millions of worlds. Life on many of them has not yet evolved into intelligent life. On some of them it never can. To be sure, most such worlds are not as desirable as ones that look just like Earth; they do not have environments in which man could live without the support of advanced technology. By the time Mars and Venus have been colonized, and starships have been developed, the technology will be available. People who dislike artificial environments, and are expecting to find a primeval paradise in some other solar system where they can "live off the land," may have to decide whether they would rather use technology or wipe out another sentient race. It is to be hoped that it will not be a very hard choice.

In the nineteenth century people resisted the thought of planets without native sentient life because they assumed those planets would be "wasted." Thomas Dick, in 1838, expressed the typical view as follows: "Now, can we for a moment imagine that the vast extent of surface on such magnificent globes is a scene of barrenness and desolation; where eternal silence and solitude have prevailed, and will for ever prevail . . . where nothing appears but interminable deserts, diversified with frightful precipices and gloomy caverns; where no vegetable or mineral beauties adorn the landscape; where no trace of rational intelligences is to be found throughout all their wastes and wilds . . . ?"

To suppose that this was the case would, in his eyes, require a "most gloomy and distorted" concept of reality. But Dr. Dick's view was narrow. He had ideas he did not know how to deal with. "Some," he admitted, "may be disposed to insinuate that the Deity may have designs in view, in the creation of matter, of which we are altogether ignorant." On the same page he said, "It is the ultimate design . . . that this world shall, ere long, be fully peopled with inhabitants . . . and this extension of population and of cultivation is evidently going forward with rapid progress at the present time in different quarters of the globe." He did not guess, in 1838, the implications of rapid progress in the extension of population, much less the connection with "empty and useless" planets.

Today, though most religious leaders see nothing contrary to religion in the concept of other intelligent beings, they are more divided on the question of space travel. Many favor it, but some are opposed. Those who oppose it may, like C. S. Lewis, be thinking of what man might do to alien races. Certainly that is a valid reason for opposition if one assumes that mankind will not gain in maturity before reaching the stars. It may be, however, that starships are too advanced an invention for a people not ready to make good use of them. That is something no one yet knows. But it is worth asking what lifeless solar systems *are* good for, if no sentient species colonizes beyond its own.

Such questions need not necessarily be answered in religious terms, at least not "religion" of the kind involving faith in a Deity. Most human beings feel that there is a reality larger than the realities of Earth, and that somehow, man fits into this universal reality. Commentators on Soviet space achievements have remarked that the people of Russia show what one writer has called "a deep and in some ways spiritual conviction that man has a significant destiny away from his home planet." That conviction is common to people everywhere, whether they believe in formal religion or not. It is in itself a form of faith: faith in mankind's future.

Our human race is, in the opinion of most scientists, younger than average. It is thought that our galaxy contains many that are thousands or even millions of years more advanced. Have these races already colonized most of the empty planets? Or if not, will there nevertheless come a time when all the countless worlds of other stars have been settled? Perhaps, if there are supercivilizations, or even a single galaxy-wide association, it does not matter who possesses which world. Yet unless the different sentient species can intermarry and have children—which is unlikely when they have evolved separately—there can never be actual merging; each human race must have its own destiny, however closely they may unite in friendship. And if expansion is necessary to evolution, a supercivilization too would have to expand. Could the entire galaxy become overpopulated?

That does not seem likely if, as some scientists have speculated, civilizations learn to thrive in the depths of space itself, no longer depending on planets any more than land animals now depend on the sea in which they first evolved. Perhaps vast cities orbit certain suns; perhaps the most highly evolved beings tap other energies, and do not need sunlight at all. Expansion, however, is more than a matter of room to live in. It demands new frontiers. Can they be found through intergalactic travel, maybe? There are billions of galaxies, but the distances between them are awesome, and the others might be as fully settled as ours.

Still, the entire universe is expanding. The galaxies are receding from each other. Some astronomers believe more are continuously coming into being. There is much not yet known about cosmology: questions of beginnings and endings, in space and in time—science has barely begun to probe the mysteries of them. They are questions for the future. There will always be more questions.

For now, people of today, like those of earlier ages, can only look up at the other suns and wonder. What is happening there? To scientists that question is pointless, for starlight spans time as well as space; a star three hundred seventy-four light-years away is seen in 1974 as it actually was in the year of Giordano Bruno's death. A radio message from its solar system would tell what its civilization was like *then*, and no doubt that civilization has since changed as much as Earth's. It is hard to think of past centuries as real; yet stars appear only as they were in the past. Can man learn to communicate across years as well as distance?

It has been suggested (and not only in science fiction) that the one thing that can travel faster than light is thought—that telepathic communication might be instantaneous. This is too speculative an idea to consider seriously at present. But the implications of it are interesting to imagine when equally unknowable areas are considered; it is no more speculative than ideas about civilizations that have had interstellar contacts for millenia.

Thoughts may not reach from one solar system to another, but thoughts *about* extrasolar worlds are the sole form of contact mankind has had, so far, with whatever life may exist beyond Earth. The ability to think such thoughts distinguishes man from other terrestrial species; it is in itself a step toward the stars, perhaps the most crucial step. About fifty years ago the author of an article about astronomy wrote: ''The knowledge that we inhabit, not this green earth alone, set in shining seas, but the wide universe, is a rightful part of the heritage of man. . . . Beasts and birds rejoice in the sunlight . . . but none of them, save man alone, looks beyond this earth to the outer immensities. Beasts and birds inhabit the world. Only man inhabits the universe.''

Man—and elsewhere, beings who live under the light of other

suns, yet look upon ours with longing. The nineteenth-century poet and novelist George Meredith expressed this feeling about the stars:

> The great life they hold,
> In them to come, or vaster intervolved,
> The issues known in us, our unsolved solved . . .
> We who reflect those rays, though low our place,
>   To them are lastingly allied.
>
> So may we read, and little find them cold:
> Not frosty lamps illumining dead space,
> Not distant aliens, not senseless Powers.
> The fire is in them whereof we are born;
> The music of their motion may be ours.
> Spirit shall deem them beckoning Earth and voiced
> Sisterly to her, in her beams rejoiced.

Science cannot say it that well. But science may someday prove it to be true.

Because length considerations make it impossible to include either formal notes or a bibliography in this book, the sources of the quotations are incorporated in the index. References to quotations or direct parapharases appear in boldface, followed by the source. The sources of quotations for which neither the author's name nor the name of the publication is given in the text are listed at the end of the index, ordered by page number. In all cases specific page citations are omitted from source data.

Adams, John, **70:** *Diary and Autobiography.* Edited by L.H. Butterfield. (Cambridge: Belknap Press of Harvard University, 1961)

Addison, Joseph, 59–60; **60:** *The Spectator.* Edited by Donald H. Bond. (Oxford University Press, 1961)

Aristotle, 15, 17–18

(Bartlett, M.R.), **67–68:** *Young Ladies' Astronomy. A Concise System of Physical, Practical and Descriptive Astronomy: Designed Particularly for the Assistance of Young Ladies in that Interesting and Sublime Study;though well Adapted to the Use of Common Schools.* (Utica, New York: Colwell and Wilson, 1825)

Bentley, Richard, 55; **55–56:** "A Confutation of Atheism from the Origin and Frame of the World, Sermon VIII" in *Works.* Edited by Alexander Dyce. (London: Francis MacPherson, 1838 — AMS Press facsimile edition, 1966)

Berkeley, George, **60:** *The Guardian* No. 70 in *British Essayists,* Vol. XIV. Edited by Alexander Chalmers. (London: Rivington, 1823)

Blackmore, Sir Richard, **12, 46:** "Creation" in *Works of the English Poets from Chaucer to Cowper.* Edited by Alexander Chalmers. (London, 1910)

Bode, Johann, 147–48, 149

Bolingbroke, Henry, Lord, **61:** "Letters and Essays Addressed to Alexander Pope, Esq." in *The Works of Lord Bolingbroke in Four Volumes.* (London: Henry G. Bohn, 1844 — Reprints of Economic Classics facsimile edition, 1967)

Brewster, Sir David, 85–88, 95–96; **86-87, 90, 103-04:** *More Worlds than One. The Creed of the Philosopher and the Hope of the Christian.* (London: Chatto and Windus, n.d.); 149

British Review and London Critical Journal, **80:** "Dr. Chalmer's Discourses" in Vol. 10 (Aug. 1817)

Drake, Frank, **120, 125–26:** quoted in "Is There Life Out There?" by Charles C. Renshaw, *National Wildlife,* Vol. 10 (Oct./Nov., 1972); 136, 138, 139, 142; **145:** "A Message from Earth," *Science,* Vol. 175 (Feb. 25, 1972); **148:** "Radio Search for Extraterrestrial Life" in *Current Aspects of Exobiology.* Edited by G. Mamikunian and M.H. Biggs. (New York: Pergamon Press, 1965)

Dwight, Timothy, **77:** *Theology, Explained and Defended, in a Series of Sermons.* (Glasgow: Blackie & Son, 1842)

Eddington, Sir Arthur, **111–12:** "Man's Place in the Universe," *Harper's Magazine,* Vol. 157 (Oct. 1928)

Emerson, Ralph Waldo, **90–91:** "Astronomy" in *Young Emerson Speaks: Unpublished Discourses on Many Subjects.* Edited by Arthur C. McGiffert, Jr. (Boston: Houghton Mifflin, 1938 — Kennikat Press reprint, 1968)

Ferguson, James, **66–67:** *An Easy Introduction to Astronomy for Young Gentlemen and Ladies.* (Philadelphia: Benjamin Warner, 1819)

Flammarion, Camille, 113; **134:** *Dreams of an Astronomer.* Translated by E.E. Fournier d'Albe. (New York: D. Appleton, 1923)

Fontenelle, Bernard de, 42; **43–45:** *A Plurality of Worlds.* Translated by John Glanvill. (London: 1688 — Nonesuch Press facsimile edition, 1929); 59, 60, 66, 70, 76

Franklin, Benjamin, **69–70:** *Papers of Benjamin Franklin.* Edited by Leonard W. Laboree. (New Haven: Yale University Press, 1963); **70:** *Writings of Benjamin Franklin.* Edited by Albert Henry Smyth. (New York: Macmillan, 1905)

Freneau, Philip, **71:** *The Poems of Philip Freneau, Poet of the American Revolution.* Edited by Fred Lewis Pattee. (New York: Russell & Russell, 1963 — reprint of 1902 edition)

Galileo, 7, 20; **32:** "The Starry Messenger" in *Discoveries and Opinions of Galileo.* Edited by Stillman Drake. (New York: Doubleday Anchor Books, 1957); 34–35, 36, 39–40

Gambol, Robert, **64:** "The Beauties of the Universe" quoted in *The Rhetoric of Science: a Study of Scientific Ideas and Imagery in Eighteenth-Century English Poetry* by William Powell Jones. (Berkeley: University of California Press, 1966)

Goddard, Robert, **115:** "Material for an Autobiography" in *The Papers of Robert H. Goddard.* Edited by Esther C. Goddard. (New York: McGraw-Hill, 1970); 178

Grasso, Domenico, **168:** quoted in *Man Among the Stars* by Wolfgang D. Muller. (London: George G. Harrap & Co., 1958)

Herschel, Sir John, **86–87:** *Proceedings of the Royal Society of London,* Vol. 16 (1867)
Herschel, Sir William, 74–75
Huygens, Christian, 46; **47–51:** *The Celestial Worlds Discover'd: or, Conjectures Concerning the Inhabitants, Plants and Productions of the Worlds in the Planets.* (London: 1698 — Frank Cass & Co. facsimile edition, 1968); 58, 70, 73, 76, 131
Hynek, J. Allen, **174-75:** quoted in *Symposium on Unidentified Flying Objects.* Hearings before U.S. Congress House Committee on Science and Astronautics. (Washington: U.S. Government Printing Office, 1968)

Jeans, Sir James, **110–11:** *The Mysterious Universe.* (Cambridge University Press, 1932) *The Universe Around Us.* (New York: Macmillan, 1929); 112, 121
Jefferson, Thomas, 70

Kant, Immanuel, 72–73; **72:** *Kant's Cosmogony, As in his Essay on the Retardation of the Rotation of the Earth and his Natural History and Theory of the Heavens.* Edited by Willy Ley. (New York: Greenwood Publishing Corp., 1968 — reprint of 1900 translation by W. Hastie); **73:** quoted in *The Great Chain of Being* by Arthur O. Lovejoy. (Cambridge: Harvard University Press, 1936)
Kepler, Johannes, 35; **36–37:** *Kepler's Conversation with Galileo's Sidereal Messenger.* Translated by Edward Rosen. (New York: Johnson Reprint Corp., 1965); 39, 64
Kipling, Rudyard, **134:** "To the True Romance" in *The Seven Seas.* (New York: D. Appleton, 1905)

Lamm, Norman, **170:** "The Religious Implications of Extraterrestrial Life," *Tradition, A Journal of Orthodox Jewish Thought* (Spring, 1966)
Lewis, C.S., **164, 171:** "Religion and Rocketry" in *The World's Last Night and Other Essays.* (New York: Harcourt Brace, 1960); 189
Lomonosov, Mikhail, **76:** "Evening Meditations on Seeing the Aurora Borealis" in *Anthology of Russian Literature* by Leo Wiener. (New York: Benjamin Blom, 1967 — reprint of 1902 edition)
London Daily News, **84:** quoted in "Speculators Among the Stars, Part II," *Blackwood's Magazine,* Vol. 76 (Oct. 1854)

Lucretius, **15:** *On the Nature of Things*. Translated by H.A.J. Munro. (London: G. Bell & Sons, 1932)

Maeterlinck, Maurice, **113:** *The Life of Space*. Translated by Bernard Miall. (New York: Dodd, Mead & Co., 1928); **114:** *The Magic of the Stars*. Translated by Alfred Sutro. (New York: Dodd, Mead & Co., 1930)

Mallet, David, **119:** "The Excursion" in *Works of the English Poets from Chaucer to Cowper*. Edited by Alexander Chalmers. (London: 1910)

Mather, Cotton, **69:** *The Christian Philosopher: a Collection of the Best Discoveries in Nature, with Religious Improvements*. (Gainesville, Florida: Scholars Facsimiles & Reprints, 1968 — facsimile of 1721 edition)

Meredith, George, **99, 192:** "Meditation Under Stars" in *Poems* (New York: Charles Scribner's Sons, 1925)

Metrodorus of Chios, 15

Milton, John, **13:** *Paradise Lost*.

More, Henry, **31:** "Democritus Platonissans, or an Essay upon the Infinity of Worlds" in *The Complete Poems of Dr. Henry More*. Edited by Alexander B. Grossart. (New York: AMS Press, 1967 — facsimile of 1878 edition)

Morrison, Philip, **136, 138:** "Searching for Interstellar Communications" in *Nature*, Vol. 184 (Sept. 19, 1959); 155

Newbery, John, 65–66; **[66:]** *The Newtonian System of Philosophy, Explained by Familiar Objects in an Entertaining Manner for the Use of Young Persons* by Tom Telescope. (London: J. Walker [and others], 1812)

Newcomb, Simon, **100–01:** *Popular Astronomy* (New York: Harper & Bros., 1882)

Newton, Sir Isaac, 35, 41-42; **42:** quoted in *Bartlett's Familiar Quotations,* 14th edition; 50; **55:** *Opticks*. (New York: Whittlesey House, 1931 — facsimile of 1730 edition); **55:** quoted in *Newton's Philosophy of Nature: Selections from his Writings*. Edited by H.S. Thayer. (New York: Hofner Publishing Co., 1953); 63

Oersted, Hans Christian, **91:** *The Soul in Nature, with Supplementary Contributions*. Translated by Leonora and Joanna B. Horner. (London: H.G. Bohn, 1852 — Dawsons of Pall Mall facsimile edition, 1966)

QUOTATIONS NOT IDENTIFIED IN THE TEXT

Page 4: "The Plurality of Worlds and Sir David Brewster," *Dublin University Magazine*, Vol. 44 (Aug. 1854)

Page 8: "Concerning the Philosophical Foundation of One Question" by I.G. Perel, *Soviet Astronomy*, Vol. 32 (Sept./Oct. 1958)

Page 63: "Merlin" by Jane Brereton, quoted in *The Rhetoric of Science: a Study of Scientific Ideas and Imagery in Eighteenth-Century English Poetry* by William Powell Jones. (Berkeley: University of California Press, 1966)

Page 79: "The Gospel its own Witness" in *The Complete Works of the Rev. Andrew Fuller, with a Memoir of his Life.* (London: G.&J. Dyer, 1845)

Page 80: "Speculators Among the Stars, Part II," *Blackwood's Magazine*, Vol. 76 (Oct. 1854)

Page 89: "The Plurality of Worlds" by Henry J.S. Smith in *Oxford Essays, Contributed by Members of the University, 1855.* (London: John W. Parker and Son, 1855)

Page 89 — 2nd quotation: See page 4

Pages 97-98: *Alone in the Universe?* by John W. Macvey. (New York: Macmillan, 1963)

Page 102: See page 89

Page 102 — 2nd quotation: "About the Plurality of Worlds," *Knickerbocker Magazine*, Vol. 61 (May, 1863)

Pages 105–06: "Man's Place in the Universe" by Theodore T. Munger, *The Outlook*, Vol. 77 (Aug. 20, 1904)

Page 107: *A Voyage in Space. A Course of Six Lectures 'adapted to a juvenile auditory' delivered at the Royal Institution at Xmas 1913* by H.H. Turner. (London: Society for Promoting Christian Knowledge, 1915)

Page 110: "The Destiny of the Universe" by Sir Francis Younghusband, *Hibbert Journal*, Vol. 31 (Jan. 1933)

Page 115: "The Vastness of the Universe," *Living Age*, Vol. 231 (Nov. 9, 1901). Reprinted from *The Spectator*.

Page 120: *Astronomy and Astrophysics for the 1970's.* (Washington: National Academy of Sciences, 1972)

Page 126: See page 8

Pages 131–32: "The Space Ship Hokum" by Rodger L. Simons, *Catholic World*, Vol. 140 (Nov. 1934)

Page 139: See page 120

Page 146: See page 102 — 2nd quotation

Page 163: "The Astrophysical Aspect of the Search for Signals from Extraterrestrial Civilizations" by N.S. Kardashev in *Extraterrestrial Civilizations,* edited by S.A. Kaplan. (Jerusalem: Israel Program for Scientific Translation, 1971)

Page 164: George Wald in *Life Beyond Earth and the Mind of Man,* edited by Richard Berendzen. (Washington: NASA Scientific and Technical Information Office, 1973)

Page 164 — 2nd quotation: Ashley Montagu (see above)

Page 168–69: Martin Redeker, quoted in *Man Among the Stars* by Wolfgang D. Muller. (London: George G. Harrap & Co., 1958)

Page 169: *Saving Belief* by Austin Farrar. (New York: Morehouse-Barlow, 1965)

Page 169 — 2nd quotation: *God, the Atom and the Universe* by James Reid. (Grand Rapids, Michigan: Zondervan Publishing House, 1968)

Page 169 — 3rd quotation: Krister Stendahl (see page 164)

Page 170: "Of New Space and Faith" by Meir Ben-Horin, *Judaism,* Vol. 8 (Winter, 1959)

Page 177: "The General Limits of Space Travel" by Sebastian von Horner and "Radioastronomy and Communication through Space" by Edward Purcell, both in *Interstellar Communication.* Edited by A.G.W. Cameron. (New York: W.A. Benjamin, 1963)

Page 178: *The Martyrdom of Man* by Winwood Reade. (New York: E.P. Dutton, 1926 — reprint of 24th edition)

Page 182: See page 177

Page 182-83: See pages 105–06

Page 183 — 2nd quotation: "Life in the Universe" [by Agnes M. Clerke] in *Edinburgh Review,* Vol. 200 (July, 1904)

Page 190: *Soviet Space Exploration, the First Decade* by William Shelton. (New York: Washington Square Press, 1968)

Page 191–92: "Ancient and Modern Thinking" by Charles Johnston, *Atlantic Monthly,* Vol. 142 (July, 1928)

Author's Note: The above citations, which are limited to works directly quoted or paraphrased, represent only a small proportion of the source material used for this book. The information presented is based on original research in primary sources, few of which — apart from modern scientific material — have been previously cited in current discussions of man's view of extrasolar worlds. Documentation of this research in a fuller and more scholarly form is in preparation.